Commercial Real Estate

UK Commercial Property

Investors and Owners

Guide

Phumipat Sookphanich

Table of Contents

Seller Pays Down Payment

Key Takeaways

CHAPTER 5: FINANCING

What Is Commercial Property Finance?
Commercial Mortgages
Bridging Finance
Auction Finance
Portfolio Finance
Mezzanine Finance
Property Development Finance

Commercial Mortgages
How Do These Mortgage Loans Work?
How to Go About Getting a Commercial Mortgage?
Relevant Loan Terms
How Does One Get a Commercial Mortgage Loan?
Commercial Mortgage Deposit
How Much Is Need for a Commercial Mortgage Deposit?
What Is the Average Commercial Mortgage Rate?

Lenders
What Exactly Is a Business Loan?
How to Apply?
How Much Can a Small Business Loan Get Me?
Different Types of Business Loans

Property Development Finance
Property Development Finance UK
How Does It Work?
Private Property Development Finance
First-Time Property Development Finance
Building Development Loans

Bridging Finance
What Is a Bridge Loan?
How Does a Bridge Loan Work?
Examples of Bridge Loans

Introduction

The two most important things in a person's life are money and time. While they are both extremely important commodities, they are not equal. Time can create money, but money can not create time.

Happiness is something else that holds a vast significance in our lives, happiness will dictate whether we look upon our lives favorably when we are old, happiness is the thing that all humans strive for. Time spent properly gives us happiness, which means the less time we spend focused on money and sustaining ourselves, the more time we can spend living proper and fulfilling lives.

In order to spend the least time possible worrying about money, and the most time possible spent on enriching our lives, I present "Commercial Real Estate." Which when partaken in responsibly can give you steady streams of large income for the rest of your life without doing hard daily labor towards it.

As a second-generation Thai immigrant and a struggler with Autism, I never had an advantage in life. However, I always made up for this through hard work and smart money management. Through this book, I wish to teach you everything I learned so far which helped me get ahead in life, and what brought me from nothing to comfortably wealthy with little work.

If you are reading this book you might be thinking, is this really right for me? Is this something that anybody can do? Does this income method really fit my skillset? To this, I respond, without a doubt, yes!

Not only can anyone do it, but it can fit pretty any skillset. People who are good with their hands can fix up problems without hiring contractors. Kind people can use this to build strong community relationships. Nerds can spend hours researching location growth. There is a use for any skill out there in commercial real estate, and even if you can't find a use for any of your skills, simple hard work can make you rich.

One of the most important things to know about Commercial Real Estate is that it is classified as "passive income." There are 2 types of income: passive income, and active income.

Active income is described as doing an amount of work within a set timeframe to make money. A waiter has to bring food to a table in a reasonable timeframe to get paid because a waiter has to be directly involved in every pound made.

Passive income oftentimes requires initial effort to start the income-generating process, but once the initial effort is completed requires little to no effort afterward. The money generated requires little to no direct involvement in making passive income.

Of these two the most appealing is passive income, nobody would turn down the opportunity to have effortless income streams, but rarely are people willing to put the effort into setting one up.

If you are willing to put a couple of months' work into having a large, effortless cash flow for the rest of your life, this is for you.

A question you might be asking is "what is commercial real estate?" The answer to that is property exclusively used for business purposes or related to providing a workspace rather than a living space.

There are many different forms of passive income, this raises the question of "why should I invest in commercial real estate?" To this, I would point out the 6 biggest pros to investing in commercial real estate: income potential, professional relationships, mutual interest between tenant and landlord, limited hours of operation, objective price evaluation, and triple net leases.

Income potential is probably the greatest reason to choose commercial real estate over other options. This can be seen with the annual rate of return which is on average 6-12%, much higher than most other options.

Building professional relationships is often overlooked in this world as a necessary skill for a business person. Having strong relationships with influential business owners can make fundraising, running for offices, and advocacy much easier. By developing real estate in your city you can build relationships with all of the businesses you rent to and develop property around.

Mutual interest between tenant and landlord is an aspect of commercial real estate which makes your entire process much easier. One of the most important things for price evaluation is how presentable and usable it is for business purposes. While people living in residential real estate are only interested in living in the property and not making it look presentable to everyone else that comes in every day, it is within the interest of business owners to make their building presentable and develop to all modern standards, this makes your life as a landlord much easier.

The limited hours of operation for businesses give great convenience to an investor, all duties including most emergencies take place during business hours. This is different from residential real estate where you could be woken up in the middle of the night to deal with major stressful issues or internet blogs where you have to work through the night writing to make sure you're on top of the trends.

Objective price evaluations are an aspect of commercial real estate that is often overlooked. While with residential real estate there are many places you can go wrong with evaluations such as being unsure of how many tenants you could get, unstable development in the area, and difficulty knowing how many apartments or houses in the area are being built. Commercial real estate, however, is fairly stable. If you hire a good broker then the price evaluations you get before purchasing your property are typically very accurate.

The final reason why you should choose commercial with real estate is because of "triple net leases." This is the most common form of the lease with business owners is a triple net lease, where the business owner is not only responsible not only for rent but to pay for property tax, insurance, and maintenance allowing you to cut the major costs of real estate investment by a large amount.

There are definitely a lot of pros to draw you into commercial real estate investment, but like with everything in this world, there are cons. These include risk, expenses to maintain the business, and a need for a large initial investment.

There are a lot of risks that lie within commercial real estate investment, while you can always get a very good and accurate evaluation of the property, many things out of your control can cause you to take a major financial loss. While there are ways to mitigate risk, something like a pandemic coming around causing businesses to close and making legislation be passed that grant massive grace periods to businesses that cannot pay their lease can always happen and there is nothing that you could do to prevent losses.

A note to make is that all investment comes with risk, while we will discuss risk management later, the point I am making is that commercial real estate can NOT replace something like a retirement fund which is meant to be stable and guaranteed.

Another issue is that you will have to spend money to maintain your commercial real estate unless you are a professional. While making money when you have a successful client and a good financial year is pretty much guaranteed, you will likely not be able to pocket the entire difference between loan payments and rent money. A commercial real estate owner needs to spend money on lawyers, some building maintenance, business management help, and tax help.

The last and possibly most challenging issue is the initial capital needed. While you will likely take out a loan worth hundreds of thousands of pounds, you need a down payment on your loan and a few months' payments in case you struggle to find a tenant. It is also helpful to renovate property immediately after buying to make it more appealing to possible tenants and to raise the value of the property.

This initial investment is something that everyone struggles with including myself, when you are young is when you should be getting ahead in life through investments like this. The issue is that it takes a lot of hard work to make that kind of money in the first place, and the restraint to invest it all instead of indulging yourself is difficult to find in a young adult. There are thousands of money management courses out there, this will only be viewed briefly in this book because money management is much more of a personal finance issue than a property investment issue, so find the right course for you and learn as much as you can while you are young, it will go a long way.

This book will spend 7 chapters preparing you for fighting in the world of commercial real estate as well as refreshing the minds of experienced individuals about modern strategies and problem-solving. By the end of this, you will know how, where, and when to invest as well as why you should do it.

Chapter 1: Understanding the Core Basics and Fundamentals

Robert Reffkin, CEO of Compass, a real estate company describes commercial real estate as "a property that is used exclusively for business or workplace purposes or to generate cash flow in some way for the owner or lessee". He also states that commercial real estate is governed by zoning, where certain types of commercial properties, such as industrial buildings, have to exist within their designated zones. Commercial real estate spaces include office space, industrial properties, multi-family residential rental buildings containing more than five units, and retail spaces. Most commercial real estate properties are owned by investors who lease the property out to relevant businesses for longer than residential real estate leases, lasting from about five to ten years.

There is a clear and distinct difference between commercial and residential real estate that needs to be made.

- The purpose of commercial real estate is to provide a place for the tenant to generate income, residential real estate obtains income by providing living space and charging a tenant to stay there.

- Lease length is also a difference, residential properties charge every month typically. However, commercial real estate typically works on five to ten years leases, a much longer period.

- Another clear difference is the zoning and location. The UK classifies the district as commercial because they intend for goods to be exchanged in that area. While residential areas are intended for people to live there and neighborhoods to be built. Residential areas typically lie on the outside areas of a city (mixed-use which is residential on top of commercial being an exception) and commercial property is typically within the heart of a city where there are a lot of people walking by often.

Commercial real estate has 8 different types: multifamily, office, industrial, retail, hospitality, mixed-use, land, and special purpose.

Multifamily Real Estate

Multifamily real estate is a cross between residential and commercial real estate. The reason it is classified as commercial is that while it is a living space, the primary purpose is for the landlord to generate profit.

The most common types of multifamily real estate are:

- Duplex, Triplex, and Quadplex: Rental properties are divided into two-unit, three-unit, and four-unit homes. These types of buildings are available in nearly every market. It's not uncommon for individual investors to live in one unit while renting out another. This is a good opportunity for someone in their mid-twenties to build friendships with tenants while paying off the mortgage on a property. This likely has the lowest initial costs among all the coming multi-family types.

- Garden Apartments: Low-rise rental apartment buildings that typically offer tenants shared outdoor space, yards, or gardens. Garden apartments are typically in the suburbs but can be anywhere. These apartments require more equity than student housing but are still very available to individuals with stable incomes that have saved up money for a while.

- Mid-Rise Apartments: Multifamily rental apartment buildings with at least 5 or more stories and an elevator, which are generally located in urban areas. These apartments require a bit more capital to buy but are a great option for those who have been in the industry for a while.

- High-Rise Apartments: Multifamily rental apartment buildings with at least 10 or more stories and an elevator, which are generally located in larger, more densely populated markets. Most high-rise apartments have over 100 units, with professional management overseeing leases and maintenance. These require a large amount of capital to put a downpayment on and are a strong option for wealthier individuals looking to diversify their portfolios.

- Walk-Up: An apartment building with 4-6 stories, and by definition, no elevator. These apartments usually have cheaper rent than mid-rise and require less initial capital. However, they are less stable which brings greater risk.

- Student Housing: Properties built specifically for student use in areas close to colleges and corresponding downtown areas. Many have large common areas. This type of multi-family real estate has very steady demand and since many college students still receive aid from their parents you can often count on a cosigner to make up for the money a student can not pay. Since there is steady demand there is usually great competition meaning that in a year with fewer students living off-campus you may have to lower rent costs to bring in tenants.

- Senior & Assisted Living: Properties built specifically for seniors, which are normally in neighborhoods where elderly populations reside. These are typically high maintenance and have high initial costs and many new tenants coming in, but the money is typically very stable with pensions, savings accounts, and government aid to the elderly.

The advantages of multi-family real estate are very clear.

There is a great diversity in what is available in this category as seen by the many different classifications listed above.

This has a very low barrier to entry, even being five to ten thousand pounds at the lowest. Making it a great opportunity for beginner real estate investors.

Geographic diversity helps mitigate risks, everywhere in the world will need affordable housing. If you can buy multiple properties in multiple cities then the chances of natural disasters or political/capitalistic foul play causing financial disaster can be mitigated or outright prevented.

Multiple income streams are possibly the greatest advantage. In retail, office, or industrial real estate you typically have one tenant per property. If that tenant goes out of business then you can go months or years without income coming from that property at all. This is in contrast to the multi-family real estate where if one of your tenants leaves you still have multiple other people paying to live there which can mitigate or even eliminate the financial problems coming from losing a tenant.

Disadvantages that you have to look out for include:

With the management-intensive nature of these properties, when there is an issue with maintenance or tenant disputes which can often happen you will be the one expected to resolve these problems.

Leases on these properties are typically renewed after one year or have monthly rent. This is in contrast to the 3-5 year leases that are often on office or retail properties.

Competition is the last main problem. To defeat competition you will have to find ways to increase the value you are providing to tenants while minimally increasing the cost to rent or lease the property.

If any of the disadvantages impact you significantly because of special circumstances then this type of real estate might be something you avoid. But if this is not the case or the advantages stick out to you a lot then this type of real estate may be for you.

Office Buildings

Office buildings are places for businesses to generate revenue, the difference between this and retail is this is primarily a space for the business to hold its employees during work time. This is not primarily a place for customers to regularly enter and exit.

There are three categories of office real estate: class a, class b, and class c.

- **Class A** is the best in terms of construction and location
- **Class B** has quality construction with a less desirable location
- **Class C** has lower quality construction and an unfavorable location

Each category of office real estate has its perks and downsides in using and owning. Oftentimes the way you either begin owning or begin leasing a type of building is based entirely on circumstance.

There are two main types of office buildings based on their location: central business district and suburban office buildings.

- Central business district (CBD) office buildings are built within the heart of cities. Large cities will often build large high-rise office buildings in the heart of their towns, these are classified as CBD office buildings.

- Smaller cities typically build large office buildings on the perimeter of the city, these buildings typically are within 7.5-75 thousand square meters.

Advantages to owning office buildings are very different from multi-family but they are still abundant.

The leases for office buildings are typically very long compared to residential housing. Some leases can range from 3-5 years while others can be up to 15-20 years. The ability to have consistent long-term income is a very strong positive. Though some extra initial effort will be needed to land a lease like this.

Another very positive thing about the leases is the fact that you can land triple net leases. Recall the earlier definition presented on this being "a triple net lease is where the business owner is not only responsible not only for rent but to pay for property tax, insurance, and maintenance allowing you to cut the major costs of real estate investment by a large amount."

The last major pro to this form of real estate requires some skill to take advantage of, but when done right can lead to a major appreciation of value. This advantage is the location of office buildings. Since most suburban office buildings are built away from major city centers the land can be relatively cheap compared to other investments. Another factor that can lead to a great increase in land value is that when thriving businesses occupy your building that incentivizes other buildings and companies to enter the area due to wealthy traffic flow consistently entering the area. In thriving cities the borders naturally lengthen as well, which means the land you own will naturally get closer to the city center as well leading to long-term slower appreciation, while this appreciation is slower it still exists and can bring great benefits.

Disadvantages just like multi-family disadvantages can be devastated when not avoided intelligently, these disadvantages include the following.

Rental rates naturally fluctuate with the economy, this fluctuation is called the real estate cycle. Both you and your tenants will likely understand the real estate cycles and they will want to decide on rent when the rates are lower and you will want to decide on the rate when it's higher. Luckily when it's higher that means the economy is prospering and many new businesses will be forming, but this does not mean you will get good rates handed to you so make sure when leasing you give rates intelligently.

Fewer income streams are also a big disadvantage. Many office buildings will have just one tenant which means if they go out of business you will have no income coming from that building and you will have to find another way to cover the mortgage and taxes on that property. Even if you rent your office space to multiple tenants there will almost always be one major tenant who if lost sometimes can not have that lost income covered by the smaller tenants.

The last thing you have to watch out for is obsoletism, if your property is old or has some other problems that make it so the building does not meet the standards of the industry that is succeeding in your area, it can lose a lot of value very quickly. Such as if the electrical capacity is low and the tech industry in your area is booming your building provides little to no value to them making it obsolete.

If any of the disadvantages impact you significantly because of special circumstances then this type of real estate might be something you avoid. But if this is not the case or the advantages stick out to you a lot then this type of real estate may be for you.

Industrial Real Estate

Industrial real estate varies greatly and often has very specific use cases. There are four major types of industrial real estate: heavy manufacturing, light assembly, flex warehouse, and bulk warehouse.

Heavy manufacturing is a very specific use type of real estate. A car production facility can not switch to a food packaging plant without a lot of capital investment.

Light assembly is a lot less specific in use but still requires capital investment and time in order to switch uses.

Flex warehouse is a very easily converted type of building that often is mixed-use with both office space and industrial buildings.

Bulk Warehouses are very large, typically 4.5-100 thousand square meters. These properties are often regional distribution plants built on highways on the outskirts of a city.

Industrial real estate typically requires large initial investments but when you manage to pay that investment the rewards are large and very stable.

Advantages to owning industrial buildings are immense due to the nature of this property just as the disadvantages are very clear. Industrial real estate is a category that is not inclusive to all and you need to be very careful before entering this type of CRE.

An advantage is the possibility of high rent yield, it is not uncommon for properties to obtain up to 10% yield while other forms of CRE can get 5-8%.

Maintenance in industrial CRE is the opposite of multi-family real estate as most of the maintenance work will be the responsibility of your tenant. This is very convenient for those who wish to take a hands-off approach.

Triple net leases are also very common in this field, which helps with both the hands-off nature and it helps you take home much more money than you normally would.

Disadvantages can encompass a large amount of the population so be very picky in this category of CRE.

A large initial cost in time and money exists in industrial real estate. A lot of industry research, capital investment, and other necessities exist for you to be successful in this area. Especially the initial time investment can be problematic since a lot of this research will amount to no purpose, you have to be a very patient person in order to succeed in industrial real estate.

Hiring professional help is also a must in industrial real estate. This likely includes property managers, legal help, maintenance, security, accountants, etc. While most clients will take over some of this professional hiring, you will have to do a lot of this yourself. It will also be your responsibility to look over these individuals and make sure they are doing a good job.

Risk is also a very prevalent factor in industrial CRE. If your client goes out of business it might take years for another tenant to come around and use the equipment you own. The loss of income from a tenant going out of business can be devastating.

Retail Buildings

Retail real estate is one of the most common forms of commercial real estate with 5 main types: strip/shopping center, community retail center, power center, regional mall, and out parcels.

An important term to know when entering the retail center is anchor tenants. Anchor tenants usually have strong brand names and pay for larger spaces. While they usually buy larger and are very stable they expect to be given privileges that smaller and less reputable tenants don't usually get: such as a say in what other tenants rent, less rent than others pay per square feet, etc.

Strip shopping centers typically are made up of small shops, such as restaurants and local stores. Though sometimes large big named stores can be found in this category.

Community retail centers are typically 40-70 thousand square meters and are made up of larger but not the largest tenants. Many anchor tenants will lease from community retail centers.

Power centers are large outdoor shopping malls that usually contain 3 or more anchor tenants. They are built with large shared parking lots entirely for the convenience of motorists.

Regional malls are the largest retail centers containing many anchor tenants and typically are in the hundreds of thousands of square meters range.

Out parcels are large pieces of land set aside for individual tenants usually being the largest in the retail center such as Walmart and Tesco. They vary in size based on location and other retail stores in the area.

Advantages and disadvantages to investing in retail real estate are likely to change in the coming future as retail is a fairly uncertain sector at the moment.

Retail real estate has been a proven sector for many years.

Retail is a very hands-off type of building to own, it is in the interest of the tenant to provide a clean and well-maintained building for their customers.

With Covid rates decreasing and people leaving their homes, more growth should be expected in the retail sector.

Retail buildings are very multi-purpose with many possible tenants available, the chances of going years in a modestly sized retail building without a tenant are very low.

Disadvantages to retail buildings have been rising more since the age of the internet began.

Specialized retail shops have been becoming obsolete outside of a few sectors since the rise of Amazon and other large online retailers. The future of in-person retail will be uncertain for a while.

Changes to the area around you can be detrimental to the real estate you own. If other large stores leave your area, air pollution largely occurs, or local infrastructure worsens the value of your property can decrease.

Hotels

Hotels vary greatly in how affordable and stable they are based primarily on location and abundance. Popular tourist areas are typically very stable but are also not very affordable. This is because the land would be very expensive and large hotel chains which are the most abundant in these areas would not wish to lease from anything other than a very large and expensive building. While smaller less tourist-popular cities would be much cheaper to own a hotel in, it would also be a much less stable income.

There are three main categories of hotels: full service, limited service, and extended stay hotels.

Full-service hotels are built in business districts and are typically the big brands such as Four Seasons, Marriott, etc. These types of hotels provide large amounts of amenities to their customers.

Limited service hotels provide fewer amenities and are less branded hotels.

Extended stay hotels typically have a kitchen and other necessities within them and provide little to no amenities. These hotels are meant to house guests for a week or more but are not meant to serve as a hotel. These are typically not very popular brands and are built outside of the main city districts.

Advantages in owning hotel real estate can vary greatly based on the type of hotel you invest in. There, however, are still commonalities that can be used as an overall metric of pros and cons.

Lodging is a relatively stable industry, with a wide variety of types of hotel real estate that can be invested in.

There is potential for very high returns if you invest in the right hotel at the right time.

The data regarding hotel investment is very accessible to the public making decisions on what to invest in and where to invest a lot less time-consuming for many parts of the process.

Diversity in location for hotels is another great advantage, you can typically find hotels everywhere in the UK. However, the size of a hotel is very dependent on the size of the city, meaning you might not be able to invest in the size you want depending on where you want to invest.

Disadvantages for hotel real estate are typical of the stability type.

The amount of money made by the hotels and by you is very dependent on the market as a whole. While vacations and visiting the family always occur, people are much more likely to take a vacation and spend less frugally when the economy as a whole is very good.

The other big issue is the constantly evolving consumer tastes, in the hotel industry the customers are always expecting new and better things which means that if you want to stay on the top of the hotel game you need to keep investing the money you make back into the hotel.

Mixed-Use

Mixed-use real estate has any type of business on the lower flowers and office space or residential properties on the upper floors. These types typically lie outside the major districts of big cities or are in the downtown of smaller cities. Downtown high-rise buildings are also almost always considered mixed-use but are made up of different types of businesses than smaller district mixed-use are. Mixed-use in its different types can be available to all sorts of real estate investors.

There are 4 types of mixed-use CRE: main street, live/work, residential and office, and mixed-use hotels.

The main street space is a mix of residential and commercial units in a town center. This space usually uses residential units on the top floor and retail space on the ground floor. The main street model is one of the oldest and longest-lasting examples of mixed-use real estate.

A live/work building has tenants live and work in the same building. This often looks like a business on the ground floor of the building, with apartments located on the upper floors.

A residential and office space is very similar to a live/work space except the tenants are not constrained to just those who work at the business.

A mixed-use hotel usually has a fitness center, retail area, and food and entertainment. Using a mixed-use hotel-style can make the hotel itself very profitable. It is usually higher-end/brand-name hotels that use this style.

There is a large rising demand for mixed-use CRE, this is largely due to millennials rising to dominance as leading real estate investors. The appeal to youths resides in the walkability of living on the mixed-use property, when you live downtown you don't need to drive downtown to make purchases. The overall rise in apartment buying leads to appeal, it is hard to explain the reasoning behind this but certainly, there was around a 10% increase in individuals renting apartments over the last 10 years. The last reason for the rise in demand is that businesses benefit heavily from walkability ever since the rise of the internet, appeal to convenience is one of the most important factors in the modern retail world and businesses benefit from walkable cities.

Advantages greatly vary from the other types of CRE discussed before even though they include multiple of the other categories.

A diverse tenant market exists in mixed-use properties. This can lead to more vibrant, interesting communities, which heavily improves property value. Young tenants are often looking less for the particulars when choosing a future living property, but rather for a healthy and diverse environment.

There is also a lot less risk in this type of property. Not only is demand rising greatly, but you have multiple income streams.

Sustainability is the last big advantage of mixed-use properties. American-style suburbs are very spread out and not only cost their cities the resources of maintaining a very large area but by making these less dense cities not walkable you require the use of cars which are a major pollutant. This all means governments and sustainability bills will not impact you heavily in the future.

There is one major **disadvantage** to investing in mixed-use properties which is the complexity. You will have multiple types of clients, a larger initial investment needed, a more difficult time finding a loan, and you have to invest more time in making sure both your commercial tenants and residential tenants are getting along and happy.

Land

Land is not often thought of as commercial real estate, but it is a large and vital part of the industry. The three types of land real estate are greenfield, infill, and brownfield land.

Greenfield land refers to undeveloped lands such as a farm or pastures.

Infill land is located in a city that has already been developed but is now vacant. Infill is strictly associated with the development of real estate in urban locations.

Brownfields are parcels of land previously used for industrial or commercial purposes but are now available for reuse. These properties are generally environmentally impaired, or at the least, are suspected of being so due to previous commercial uses.

Advantages to owning land real estate are very unique considering the often undeveloped nature this takes, these advantages include:

The land is relatively easy to acquire, while research, consultation, negotiation, etc. are necessary the process is often much quicker and easier for real estate of this category.

There is often little competition factor. People buy land according to their needs, and this land is often not abundant meaning people will often have to make a deal they can get.

The low cost of maintenance is probably the biggest factor to consider. While improving land is an option, intelligently bought land while likely to appreciate naturally meaning this is as passive as income gets.

Disadvantages include mainly the risk involved in this type of purchase. It is a lot easier to classify this as an investment in the local economy than an active business venture. If you are wrong regarding your prediction of the future value of this property you can lose a lot of money.

Special Purpose

Special Purpose is the last category to know and is effectively the miscellaneous category. Commercial real estate experts typically have to learn even more categories, but to the average investor, this will be all you need to cover.

When investing in something that can be classified as a special purpose you will need to do your own research and think about the pros and cons of owning such a property.

Key Takeaway

The classification of your potentially owned commercial real estate will be your first and most important step in the process of owning CRE.

When buying a property you need to first classify it, then look over the advantages and disadvantages to see how well this fits your life.

The last important thing to realize is that these broad categories do not encompass every single factor when buying commercial property. Every single property will have special implications, and you have to do your own research and brainstorming before buying the land to know that it will work for you. These categorical implications are not the entire facts for every property.

Chapter 2: Investment Strategies

After deciding on a property to buy the next step is determining how you will end up paying for the property. In order to overcome this issue, you will turn to investment strategies.

Buying a property outright is pretty much impossible for those entering the field of commercial real estate. Luckily this is not the only way to get access to the industry because there will be loans, companies, and investment funds available to beginners such as yourself. While monetary contributions from yourself will likely be expected, you do not have to be rich to enter this field.

In this chapter, we will cover the investment types of direct investments, direct commercial property funds, and indirect property funds.

Direct Investment

Direct investments make use of pure capital to get a percentage of ownership in a real estate company. This is typically unreasonable when just entering the field due to a lack of capital that can be used as a down payment for a loan.

Most real estate professionals suggest avoiding this route when entering the field of CRE especially when there are other options available.

Buy-To-Let Mortgages

Buy-to-let mortgages are the type of mortgages you will be getting in the world of CRE. The mortgage you will typically get can require 20-40% of the property value as a down payment.

You should expect to pay a large interest on a loan like this, as there is a lot of risk for the lender in this business.

A popular tactic of lenders to get their loans paid off is to charge 125% of their monthly rental income on the property as loan payment, because of this the land-owner would be operating at a loss for a while, but get their loan paid off sooner.

Commercial Property Funds

A commercial property fund consists of many investors contributing a certain amount of money to buy the property, then splitting the risk and gains evenly among themselves.

If you own 5% of a property you will gain 5% of the rent whenever it is collected. Not only this but once you decide to sell your 5% of the property you could get more money than you initially invested if the property value appreciated.

The **Lock-out** clause in many contracts in commercial property funds is something you need to closely look out for. What this clause does is allow fund managers to prevent you from selling your share in the property for up to 28 days while they collect the funds to pay back those wishing to exit the fund.

Why Commercial Property Funds?

Commercial property funds are probably the best possible option for a beginner. If you buy an entire property on your own just after entering CRE, your inexperience might lead you to not make the best decisions and without years of capital buildup from buying and collecting rent on properties, you won't have any saving grace for if you take a major loss on the property.

There is by far much less risk in commercial property funds, while you are not active in management, you still have to read the market and predict what land and in what market will rise the most in value.

Indirect Property Funds

Indirect Real Estate investments include investing in real estate companies. While you are investing in the real estate market and you can put the exact amount of capital you want at a time, you do not have the control over the property management that might be appealing to those interested in this field.

Despite the obvious downside of lack of control and no management experience gained, you still gain the skill of reading the market. The other major upside to this is how diversified the *Real Estate Investment Trusts (REITs)* are.

When investing in indirect property funds you are not investing in individual properties, but rather the market as a whole.

Investment Funds

Investment funds (aka mutual funds) have large prebuilt portfolios which are heavily diversified and you play no role in which companies are bought on behalf of the fund. These typically are long-term funds that average a steady rate of return in the 7-15% return rate (Gifford, 2011).

This is a great investment for your retirement account, but not something that I would recommend for a youth investor trying to make big money.

Unit Trusts are a subcategory of investment funds in which a fund manager buys and sells stocks or bonds in real estate companies and separates them into units. These units are evaluated often and that value is always presented to you before you buy them.

If you are young and looking to make higher-risk investments then coordinate with a trust manager to build a high risk / high reward unit trust account. It is better to leave professionals to the everyday managing of these accounts, but it should always still be your choice in the overall theme of any investment accounts you enter into.

Open-Ended Investment Companies are built very similar to unit trusts, except they are much more centralized and structured. There is a team of high-earning experts making the decisions on what to do with each stock they work with daily and their goal is to as a company outplay the market and bring as many customers in as possible in order to earn a commission.

Trusts of both types explained above will either pay you in two ways: Income Units or Accumulation. These payments usually come either monthly, quarterly, or every 6 months.

Income units are payments of direct cash to investors of the share in profits they owned. This is a good option for those who are using trusts to build up short-term profits. If you have a larger investment such as a mortgage on a property or any other major income source.

Accumulation payment takes the share of the profit you earned and instead of paying directly in cash the company will reinvest all of that money into your trust for you. This is good for a long-term account such as a retirement or savings fund.

Investment Strategies in Practice

Our hypothetical investor will be named Goerge. Here is all the information you need to know about George.

-   34 years old
-   has £190,000 in available investment capital
-   already has a well-established retirement fund
-   owns £90,000 in commercial property funds
-   manages for a large home maintenance company
-   lives in a well off medium-sized suburban town
-   he is a talkative people person

What advice would I give George?

The first thing is identifying experience and skill set. He knows how to maintain a home very well, he has a job that does not usually require hours longer than 40 a week, while he has £60,000 available he also has £20,000 and a decent income to leverage.

Based on what I see in his portfolio, I would suggest entering multi-family real estate. He has been working hard long enough to gain the capital to buy a (smaller) property of his own.

The first thing to do is market research on his town and the neighboring towns. The town he lives in likely has a stable customer base and with the population continuously growing, the cost of real estate tends to witness favorable increases for investors.

This individual is interested in an apartment, it is one building with 5 living spaces within it. After doing weeks of research he finds a property for sale at the price of £700,000.

He decides after doing a lot of research on the property, bringing in experts to examine, consulting his bank, and doing his due diligence he finds there are no catastrophic faults in the property and begins the process of buying.

He determined that he did not have enough confidence in himself yet to stake such a large amount of money into an investment, because of this he sought out an older, experienced investor by the name of Mark.

Mark in this instance would own 30% of the property and Goerge would own 70%. They split the initial cost accordingly and had a business contract written up by a CRE attorney.

Mark has the role in this partnership of both providing capital and advice in the hope of both profiting from this endeavor.

After this, they decided to take out a loan for the property. They went with a direct investment opportunity since they had enough capital to do so and did not want to work with a major company.

After meeting with a bank they nailed down their deal for a buy-to-let mortgage where they would pay 25% down and have 6.8% interest paid off over 30 years.

Under this agreement the two combined would have to pay 175,000 pounds down, George owning 70% of the property would pay 122,550 pounds and Mark would pay 52,450 pounds. They would have a 3,422-pound monthly payment for a loan that would last 30 years. They would pay a total of 1,232,138.61 pounds meaning that they would need to collect 684.52 pounds a month from each tenant to break even on the investment. This, however, would not mean they made no money, the second they pay off the property it means they made 700,000 pounds multiplied by however it appreciated over thirty years with little to no regular monetary cost.

While this was a rough interpretation with little real-world accuracy, this shows how you would calculate the necessary rent to pay, how much the monthly payments would be, and everything regarding the initial payment process for CRE.

How Do You Decide How to Invest?

Deciding what investments would work best for you should be based on an analysis of the pros and cons of each investment.

Direct Investment

Direct investment is a great option for those with a large amount of starting capital, a stable wage, and a lot of research into their market in recent years.

The major problem with it is that most of you readers won't have the previously stated qualifications as you are just entering the field. This means that unless you have a very good loan opportunity in your area you likely won't be able to invest in this way for a few years.

If you have the initial capital and a large stable income then I would suggest investing in this way. You will likely have to get a buy-to-let mortgage, under this mortgage agreement you will typically have to put 15-40% down on your investment depending on how large the investment is and what type it is. For riskier investments, the banks you work with will want more money down and a higher interest rate on your loan. There will likely not be one loan standard for every single investment that you make (Trudeau, 2016).

Once you get the loan, do your due diligence, and get ownership of the property you will have a lot of freedom to run your property as you see fit. The freedom from co-owners is probably the greatest advantage of buying CRE like this. Not only do you get to run the property your own way, but you get to keep all of the profits as well.

Commercial Property Funds

These funds are probably the best place for someone to start investing, there is a low cost of entry, control of what property you are investing in, and considerably lower risk than direct investment.

If you are a beginner in the field or are someone looking to put a couple of thousand pounds into an investment outside of a larger investment then this is your choice.

Indirect Property Funds

This is not an option I would suggest to those looking for short-term gains, however, this is an amazing option for those confident in their real estate market and need to choose the stocks for their retirement funds. While you do not usually build up capital as fast as you would with investing directly into a property and collecting rent, it is a stable investment that will usually gain 8-12% annual returns.

Investment Funds

The greatest advantage to an investment like this is a low-time commitment with an above-average rate of returns. There is also a barrier of entry low enough to compare to commercial property funds, but you also need to invest enough capital to make it worth the time of whatever company or individual you are investing with.

A disadvantage to consider is the amount of money the trusts might charge you to gain from their expertise. While many will likely charge you an initial fee or a fixed rate, others might charge you based on the amount of money you gain with them. Based on this, if you have the time to research by yourself and make educated calls on individual properties or companies to invest in, I would suggest doing that to avoid the massive fees you will pay with a trust.

Partnerships

Partnerships are something I would highly recommend for intermediate real estate investors for your first experience managing a commercial property.

A partnership is where you work with an experienced partner and both claim a percentage of ownership in whatever property you invest in. While the senior partner will have the most control in the relationship, you will still have a responsibility in decision-making and will be able to learn a lot about how investing works in practice.

If you have enough capital to pay off at least 40% of the downpayment and a stable enough income to contribute during hardships I would heavily recommend this to you as a stepping stone into owning a property of your own.

To locate a partner, what you simply must do is find local well-known CRE investors and call them or email them.

Key Takeaways

This chapter was entirely based on all of the different ways that you can put your money into the market and how you should make your decisions based on the options presented.

What you need to remember is that circumstances are always different, the barrier of entry in a small town in the middle of nowhere will obviously be much smaller than the barrier of entry into a major city. What is considered enough capital to enter your local market will vary heavily place by place.

Something else that needs to be considered before entering a market is that the entry cost on its own is not enough to maintain ownership over the property. You need an emergency fund that is large enough to support you for several months, tenantless. The number of months that you need to be able to support tenantless will vary based on what type of property you own and how much your monthly mortgage payments are.

When you enter a market you need to remember that the old investment saying "never put all of your eggs in one basket" still applies. There will always be a risk in every investment, therefore, you need to separate your retirement account from your investment account. You also need to have multiple different investments at once, do not buy complete ownership of a property if you do not have stocks or indirect property funds that can still bring in passive income while your property faces financial troubles.

Risk should also be factored in based on your circumstances. If you are young and have enough capital either coming in or saved up to support your family then, risks bringing poor outcomes can be negated over time. However, if you lack either the required income to overcome a risk or the time before retirement to earn back lost capital, then you should not be making financial decisions that are too risky.

The last very important thing to take into account is that you never have to make these decisions alone, there are resources out there such as financial advisors and accountants that can help you make sure that you are financially capable of investing before you make it. If you have a trusted financial advisor in your family that you can go to for advice then I would say that going to them is a must. If you do not have a trusted financial advisor then finding one is a must. Most people do not have the motivation or time to learn how to act in a financially savvy way. Financial advisors use not only their college degrees but years of experience to make sure you make the best financial decisions available to you.

Chapter 3: Due Diligence

There is a checklist-like process you must do before buying any commercial property, this is called due diligence and it does an amazing job mitigating risks brought up by unforeseen issues.

Due diligence, however, far exceeds just a checklist that works for every situation. Due diligence is an investigation into the question "is there any issue or reason why a tenant would not want to rent from this property? Can that issue be resolved with a reasonable amount of money? Is there anything that would stop me from deriving profit through my intended use of this property?" If you can not find the answer to every question above, then you are not ready to buy the property.

A story to teach you why due diligence is important is about an investor in the US state of Texas.

When an investor found a large property on a famous road he could not believe himself, it was only about four million pounds which was very cheap for the road, especially because of the size of the property. There was a church on the property and he wanted to turn it from a church into a shopping center, so he looked over the property with a construction company and they gave approval, and he looked over the property with his financial advisor and he gave approval for his loan. However, he failed to look into public office records regarding the property, there had already been two attempts to rezone the property which both failed. When he brought his case before the town hall, a group of residents strongly protested against the rezoning because they lived nearby and did not want to deal with noise pollution. After fighting with his lawyer for a long time he begrudgingly put the property up for sale for the price he bought it, but nobody bought it. After dropping the price multiple times in hope of somebody buying, he ended up at the lowest he could possibly go at £800,000. Because this individual failed to consider the fact that this property might be at such a steal due to it being impossible to redistrict, he lost £3.2M.

Due diligence is extremely important, and as previously shown, if you do it properly it can save you a great deal of money over time. So, especially if it is your first time investing, do hours of research and examine every possibility even if those possibilities lie outside of the checklist.

The two types of investigations you must do are the physical and documental investigations.

The physical investigation is based on the condition of the building itself. Usually, it is suggested not to do this investigation alone as the logistical aspects might be too difficult for an everyday person to understand, good help would come from a civil engineer, former building inspector, or a carpentry company. You would need to look into how physically appealing the building is, the structural reports, how strong is the building material, and if there are any major defects to the property.

The big question will be is this building up to the standards of my possible tenants? Will my tenants look at their building with pride as the face of their brand? If one of the previously stated criteria is not met by the building the question you will ask is "is the price to fix this reason enough to make it worth purchasing the building?" Sometimes the price for fixing the building makes the purchase not worth it, and it is perfectly reasonable to turn down a building if the cost for repairs is too great.

The documentary investigation requires a lot of analytical skills, which sometimes investors do not have. This is perfectly ok, but for those people, I would suggest hiring a real estate lawyer to do this part of due diligence on their behalf. If you are not confident in your investigative skills, the best advice I can give is that the cost of hiring a lawyer is far less than the cost of a major financial loss on behalf of a bad investment.

This process involved reviewing the property's identification, its certificate of title, its zoning and use, and finally its insurance. These are the standard steps, but a good due diligence investigator will look over lease agreements, tenancy schedules, and the GST position on each lease. While it might be easy to just pour over all of these issues in an hour or two and be done with it, you must go above and beyond in your investigation into each issue. Oversights happen when an investigation is rushed, so take your time, and do not leisure during this time. While this might be a pain resembling homework in school for most people, this can be the deciding factor in whether you make hundreds of thousands of dollars or lose hundreds of thousands.

Everything comes down to whether this is a place that your tenant will want to occupy. Your tenants are the people that will pay the rent you use to pay off the loan for this property. However, protecting yourself from major unforeseen circumstances is another very large issue. This means that you will most likely end up spending half of your time determining how you can please your future tenants, and the other half of your time trying to prevent profit loss from bad circumstances. An example of this would be buying an office that requires too many repairs before it can become functional or buying an industrial property that does not have the equipment your targeted client needs to run their business.

Most of the due diligence comes down to simple critical thinking, looking over real-life examples and dreaming up hypotheticals will be a major part of your process. This process of examining hypotheticals will lead you to look over both natural disaster focused and politically focused risks. For example, a green initiative to build larger amounts of mixed-use walkable neighborhoods could force you to change your entire building designation which creates a major financial risk.

Office Properties

Office properties are unique in the way that you are working together with your tenant to create a positive and healthy work environment for your tenant's employees. This mutually beneficial relationship can be extremely valuable if you can handle it properly.

Each classification of CRE has important aspects to the property you have to look for to guarantee that they meet the standards of your future clients. Things you should look for in an office property that will attract clients are:

- Great natural light and attractive views all over the property. Keep in mind that not only will the company owners, but all of their employees will be looking at this view for 40 hours a week for years. When you are looking to buy an office property try sitting down by a window and imagine how you would feel sitting there as a worker. Also ensure there is good natural light and a good amount of natural light coming in, this is something business owners often look for in buildings.

- Amenities are a good way of sticking out from the crowd. While every office space will have cubicles and break rooms, not many have exercise rooms, showers, kitchen areas, gardens, balconies, etc. Imagine you are pitching this building to big companies, ask yourself "how can I impress the owners best?"

- Parking is a major issue in suburban offices, while in big cities parking is a good amenity. If your city is car-dependent, then you will want to have a parking capacity that is close to or equal to the building capacity.

- Building close to public transportation hubs is a major plus when your office is in a big, public transportation-reliant city. In a car-heavy city, this is a less important thing to worry about when buying an office space.

- Disability accessibility is a big plus in office spaces. While installing a concrete ramp next to outside stairs might be a relatively simple change, installing an elevator could be a lot more expensive. Consider the cost behind making a building disability accessible and the disability rates in your city before buying an office property as this can be a make or break issue.

- Ask previous or current workers at the property about their opinion of the place. There is no better judge of a property than someone who worked there. After you collect opinions try to judge how financially reasonable it would be to make the changes to the property. Setting goals for office adjustments would be a good and efficient way to raise property value.

- Air conditioning, clean water, heating, plumbing, and electricity are all modern standards for office buildings. Unless there are cheap fixes to the issue, avoid them at all costs.

Industrial Properties

Industrial properties, naturally, do not have the same standards as office properties. What you will find is logistical topics are much more heavily focused on in this type, this is because efficiency is the driving force in industrial companies. What tenants in industrial properties are looking for is:

- Drive-through accessibility, industrial trucks need a way to smoothly move in and out. If the trucks have close accessibility to the initial stocking room that is another big plus.

- Wide, truck acceptable, public roads are a must. Not only do you want to insure accessibility but you want to make the roads convenient for truckers. On some days multiple trucks can arrive and leave these properties and you want everything to go smoothly so your tenants can avoid being backed up due to the inadequacy of your lot. Another big plus is when your property is close to a highway.

- Safety is extremely important in industrial properties because in the instance of a lawsuit due to unsafe work conditions both you and your employer can be held liable. So it is best to ensure the floors have traction in all climates, railings everywhere there is a fall hazard, etc. An expert such as a personal injury lawyer or an HSE representative would be a good advisor on this issue.

Other important areas you should look into are:

- Manufacturing capabilities and that specific product's growth in your area?
- Capacity and possible companies that would need that capacity?
- Major suppliers in your area and contact numbers?
- Description of any possibly toxic chemicals used in the past or currently and all information relating to them that could cause harm to the property or your business?
- Past business agreements or leases?
- What are the future expenses relating to the manufacturing of the specialized product?
- What equipment is being leased at the property and what is the price of that equipment?
- Is the possible tenant willing to make any change to the contract terms?
- Does your possible tenant and building have good safety records?
- What are your fixed and variable costs?
- Are defective products regularly produced at this property? Where does the fault lie for those defective products being produced?
- Who are the subcontractors that are usually hired to work in this plant?

Retail Properties

While in the previous two properties you need to appeal to your tenant and their process, in the retail section you need to, through your property management, help your tenant appeal to their possible customers. You do this through:

- Having a good deal of passing cars. The rise of impulse purchasing is something that many companies are trying to take advantage of, by having the property on a busy street with an easily accessible parking lot you can take advantage of the impulsive nature of many customers. Even having a property close to another retailer can help your client, especially if that retailer belongs to a large chain.

- Convenient parking is a must, you need at least enough parking spots to fit the max store occupancy and preferably more than that. Easy access to the entrance is another major advantage to a property that your tenants will be looking for.

- Tenants will also be looking for high quality heating and A/C systems. Good electrical systems and plumbing are also a must because most stores rely very heavily on those being stable. Overall, tenants are looking for an environment that has all the essentials needed to provide an experience for their customers.

- Fit-out construction is something that most tenants are looking for. Fit-out refers to buildings with base flooring, standard white walls, standard ceiling, HVAC, plumbing, restrooms, elevator and stairs, and adaptations to local building codes. The reason that most companies prefer this rather simple building design is due to a preference for designing their stores themselves. The store a retailer operates in is their brand image after all.

Overall Checklist

While every type of property will have things that you must look at in order to guarantee success, there are some points that you can check across all building types that will be explored here.

- How long ago was the last vacancy and how long did that last?
- What are the average rental rates in this area for similar buildings?
- How will rezoning affect this building in the future
- Is the price that is trying to be claimed for this reasonable
- Are road widening or large scale plans likely in this area?
- Is this land contaminated?
- What are the tenancy trends in this area?
- What natural disasters are this building susceptible to?
- Is there ability to extract value of the land outside of the tenant? (solar panels, shipping drop off. pick-up, etc.)
- What is the legal description of the property?
- What are the third party reports that have been taken of the property?
- What do any declaration of convents, conditions, restrictions, reservations, or easements say about this property?

- What do the available income and expense reports say about the property?
- What legal issues have arisen on the property in the past? Include these in your research even if it may not seem relevant to investigation
- Where are the permits for this property?
- What is the state of building/ state of area around it?
- Does it require maintenance?
- What about the traffic report?
- What about the Certificate of Title?
- Are there any restrictions on sale?
- Will there be restrictions on lease?
- What about the rates of tax/ tax adjustments?
- Are there any undermining factors that could cause financial harm?
- Where can one get all the available history including tenancy rates, tenant turnover, historical maintenance and repairs?

Key Takeaways

When you are beyond the step of identifying the property and discovering your proper investment strategy the immediate step you need to take is identifying your due diligence checklist. Reaching out to experienced investors and investigating through online sources will give you great results, but if you want to be truly safe you must do your own research and critical thinking about what your checklist needs.

While this might sound intimidating to many, with enough effort anyone can identify what needs to be on your due diligence checklist.

The first step into your personal investigation is to ask, what would I do right now if I owned this property? Then ask yourself, how much would I gain from this? If the gains seem to be very large ask yourself, why didn't the previous owner or anyone who could have seen the property before me do this? Simply, just like with getting rich quick scams if it seems to be too good to be true, it likely is.

The next step is to use your resources to understand what your tenants will be looking for in a building and ask yourself, does this building have all of those things? If not, then ask yourself, how much time, effort, and money would it take to add on those missing aspects myself?

Remember, experts are your best friends in business. If you are tackling an issue that is outside of your league then get someone who can give professional opinions for you. If you try to tackle the world of CRE without the help of anyone you will sink and lose a lot of money.

Lease history, disabled accessibility documentations, titles, and zoning+property codes are all documents that will give you the best knowledge of what the property has been through. While consumer behavior changes, this change is not drastic enough to make the recent past irrelevant. Use every single piece of data that you can find because using the past as clues can help bring much more stability to your future.

The most important thing to remember is that very bad things happen when you do not do your due diligence, this is not something to even procrastinate over. When you have hundreds of thousands of dollars at stake, you need to enter into any deal or investment without any uncertainty.

There are hundreds of digital, human, and readable resources to help you with this process, this means that no matter the struggle an answer can always be found! Simple hard work is all you need to get through this process, finding help and understanding the advice that is given to you is a part of that hard-work. Don't be afraid to get help, and work hard through this possibly painstaking process to achieve your dreams!

leave a review

As an independent author with a small marketing budget, readers are my livelihood on this platform, If you enjoy this book so far, Id really appreciate if you left your honest feedback. You can do so by clicking the link below. I love hearing from my readers and I personally read every single review

Link to review page https://www.amazon.com/

Chapter 4: Buying Commercial Properties

Now that you know how the three main aspects of buying a property work, the next step is finding one.

A real estate agent is somebody who can be of great help in this adventure, however, these people can often be pricey so you might want to avoid spending the precious initial funds you have on them.

The purpose of this chapter will be on how to read the market, find the right property, and learn what to do once you have found that property that would work the best for you.

Analyzing the Market

As with every economic system, you will find ups and downs in your market. While you can research all of your locally available real estate as a first step before you buy anything in CRE, you want to know for sure you are buying at the right time.

By investing at the right time you can both get a very good price, as well as help you buy the property in the right place of a city that has foreseeable growth.

There are three key areas to look at which will help you predict your local market: demographics, supply and demand, as well as capital markets.

Demographics

The most experienced real estate investors who usually work for major firms will focus initially on the demographic profile of a possible investment area. This is because demographics can give you a unique insight into the human side of economics. Demographic statistics do not give you every single answer out there, rather it serves as a key to unlocking many other insights which will be useful when deciding what investment you want to make in a certain area.

Merriam-webster describes demographics as "the statistical characteristics of human populations (such as age or income) used especially to identify markets".

One of the most important statistics you will find is population growth. When you compare population growth, job growth, and buildings planned, you can fairly accurately predict what areas are going to have demand for them. You want to use these demographics to predict when demand for buildings of your type is going to be at the lowest and buy your building then.

You want to buy a building when the demand is lowest because this is when the prices are going to be lowest, little demand = lower price. The issue that naturally arises with this is the difficult nature of finding a tenant at this time. This strategy of buying a building will help to ensure that your building appreciates over time, rather than depreciates. The natural risk is not being able to find a tenant in the time that your emergency fund can cover.

Another strategy of buying a building involves predicting the highest point of demand and buying then. If you can accurately predict when demand will be highest you can enter land ownership with decent certainty that you will be able to find a tenant. The natural risk in this is that other investors will also be trying to predict when demand will be highest, this means that you could end up feeling the inflation of prices before the demand reaches its height. The worst-case scenario is that the expected demand is much higher than the actual demand, in this scenario you can end up buying a property for a higher-end price without the certainty you normally have of finding a tenant. This strategy of using demographics as a prediction is very high risk/high reward.

For new investors I suggest buying at a predicted low point, if you have the initial funds you should have when entering the CRE world then the risk can be mitigated and your investment would work out in the long term with most likely a little appreciation in property value.

Income Statistics
Income statistics have a major effect on retail stores especially, as well as residential investments.

Naturally, communities with a higher GDP per capita will have larger growth in retail properties. While this does affect when to buy in the market, I would suggest using this more to decide whether to enter a market. If you enter into the CRE market at a high point when many businesses are being created you could end up leasing to a business that fails, which brings instability into your investment. If a business continues to grow even during a recession it would likely be a very good tenant to have.

Residential CRE is different in the fact that it is easier to change tenants. Because of this, you should always be looking to decide on your lease agreement when the market is at a high point.

Key Takeaway of Demographics

When deciding on where you want to invest you want strong net-migration patterns, strong job growth, a diverse employment market, and an upward trajectory in incomes.

You want to enter the market when prices are low with a way of countering the natural risks that come with entering at that time.

Remember that entering the right market at the right time can be the difference between making 100s of thousands and making millions.

Supply and Demand

Supply and demand are the driving forces in all of economics, this includes the real estate market. We touched on supply and demand analysis in the previous section, but this will be a deeper dive into this fundamental part of the market.

Supply and demand indicators will drive you to find the time when the prices are highest and lowest possible. This will be greatly helpful for both buying and selling commercial property. The difference between supply and demand indicators and demographic indicators is that the latter gives you insight into whether the property you are interested in is set to appreciate or depreciate over a long period, while the former helps you understand what the short-term real estate prices are set to look like. In short, demographics give you a 10-30 year estimate, and supply and demand give you a 1-10 year estimate.

There are many supply indicators, the first one we will be looking at is the construction pipeline. This includes 4 different aspects: proposed projects, planned projects, projects under construction, and newly built properties.

While supply and demand are fundamentally linked together, for our purposes it is better to split these into two parts.

Using these supply indicators you can understand what the prices are going to look like in the future, however, you have to pair the knowledge you obtain with the following supply indicators to gauge what the prices of commercial property will be soon.

Supply indicators include current vacancy levels, net absorption, and historical and projected rent growth figures.

Vacancy levels show the amount of space that is available, and if there is a large amount of vacancy this means that people will be regularly lowering their leasing prices in order to bring more customers in.

Net absorption is (the total number of units/total square footage that has been occupied within a certain time frame - the total amount that became vacant) very positive net absorption means that a large amount is looking to lease shortly.

Rent growth gives you the amount of money that can be made on a given property, high rent growth means that you can expect to make a lot of money once you enter the market.

Capital Market Effect on CRE

When a large firm enters the local area, that can have major implications on your property's value in the future. When a major investment firm buys a property in your area this means they have noticed a positive trend in this area. If an unnaturally large amount of money is poured into your real estate market this could be indicative of a bubble that you would want to avoid.

On the other hand, if a large non-real estate company enters your area this could be a major positive for your market. If Google buys an office space providing 1,000s of jobs in your city this could cause a major increase in value for multifamily real estate owners due to a large amount of housing needed compared to a small amount of housing available.

With thousands of new people in the market, more restaurants may open, more retail stores may open, and more roads may need to be built, meaning money entering construction companies. A single large company entering your city could cause massive financial growth which you as a landowner would capitalize on.

Finding and Buying a Property

Once you know what market you want to enter the next steps are to find some properties that you are interested in.

Commercial real estate agents as previously stated are a good option for those looking to invest, however you are capable of finding places on your own. Just know a lot of the processes may end up being much harder for you than they would have been for others.

It is important to remember that property owners looking to sell want you to find their property, this is because the more people who see their property the more bids will be made and the more money they make.

You can usually find properties for sale on a multitude of websites, on signs by their town, and advertised on internet pages for CRE investors.

Once you find a property you are interested in, simply copy the address and plug it into your search engine. Doing this can help you find the relevant offers that have been made.

Find many different properties that match your interests, I would suggest at least ten. After finding the ten best for you, compare everything. Risks, money, amenities, places around it, etc. A good checklist to look over follows the order:

1. Find comparable properties.

2. Review the offerings.

3. Choose your investment strategy.

4. Get renovation estimates.

5. Gather term sheets from lenders.

6. Run the numbers to determine your returns.

Once you find the best property you should contact the owner of the property and ask them any questions you may have, some of which should be from your due diligence checklist. Once you ensure that the property is worth the time, effort, and money to continue onto the next steps, contact the important aids you have for your dealings. This will include your financial advisor, lawyer, banking officer, partner, mentor, etc.

Every situation will be different, at all times get advice from the experts you are working with within the steps you have to take next. However, once you decide to move beyond the initial findings part of the deal ask the owner to take the property off the market. It would be bad if another investor took away your opportunity by putting in a very high deal.

Once you have looked over every aspect of the investment and secured a loan from your bank, send in an offer on the lower end. If they refuse to enter negotiations with the help of an expert.

After obtaining the final deal, go through with your investment strategy that should have been determined before making this deal. Contact your lawyer to investigate your contract, if your lawyer does not have much experience in contract law they may end up recommending a contract lawyer to you for this part of the job.

Outside the Box Thinking for Payment

While we discussed payment strategies previously, there are some other more creative ways of paying for your property.

The difference between these and the other strategies is that these are completely dependent on the specific property itself.

These options consist of obtaining a real estate license, lease with option to buy, subject to, seller financing, and the seller pays down payment. All of these are creative options that might not always be available depending on the specific property and property owner.

Real Estate License

If you have enough time on your hands to study for the license, not only can it help you land your initial property, but it can be a useful tool for you later on.

If you have your real estate license you can recommend properties that do not work out for you to others in hope of making some money if they buy it.

When you do buy a property you might even be able to negotiate for a commission that might be up to 3% of the total cost, which could end up being 15% of your down payment (The Cauble Group, n.d.).

While this is a very strong option, it is only available to those who have the time and motivation to study hard for the licensing test.

Lease With Option to Buy

A lease with an option to buy essentially allows you to lease the property from the owner, but the money made by the lease goes toward the purchase of the property. While you are leasing the property you can operate a business out of it or sub-lease it to tenants of your own to make the payments.

This is a very good option if you can get the property owner to agree to it. A condition of the property owner might be to buy the property at an inflated price or pay a larger amount for rent than would normally be charged.

Another condition for this option is that the tenant can not be leasing the property at the moment, in this situation you must have enough money saved up to cover a few months of rent without having a tenant in the property.

Subject To

If a property owner is having financial troubles and can not pay for their mortgage you can take up their property and their mortgage on the property. You will be subject to the terms of their mortgage so you have to ensure that it is something that you can keep up with.

Something else to consider is the circumstances behind the failure of the previous owner. If they were as planned and prepared as you are you have to ask what is stopping you from sharing the fate. Be certain you completely understand everything that leads to the former owner's failure before you decide anything.

Seller Financing

If you can find a willing participant in this strategy this could be one of the best possible options.

Seller financing is where you accept debt to the former property owner rather than the bank. You will make monthly payments to the former owner until you meet the agreed price with possibly some interest. However, if you are doing a seller financing option you should either be paying a lower interest than you would be at the bank or you should have more leniency on payments.

While to the observant reader this might seem like a very bad option for the seller, on further inspection it really isn't.

This is because the seller avoids some tax obligation from the sale, they get a nice monthly income, they get to help out someone new to CRE, they can get rid of the property faster, and they could have greater returns in the long run, and much more.

Something to consider is that this is a more rare strategy, you will likely need some form of relationship with the owner for this to work.

The other important thing to remember is to keep the contract negotiation as much between your lawyers as possible. Not only do you get the best deal possible for both of you this way, but your personal relationship does not get in the way of business.

I would highly recommend this to anyone it is available to, however, those instances will be few.

Seller Pays Down Payment

If you have confidence in your ability to make your monthly payments but not enough capital to pay your down payment you can use this option.

This method lies in an agreement made between the owner of the property and the buyer. The buyer purchases the building at an inflated price and in exchange the building owner provides you the funds to pay off your down payment.

This is a good option if you managed to obtain a strong salary that can cover your monthly payments, but you did not have time or money to obtain your down payment.

The scenario above is fairly rare and unless you are one of the people that cover I would suggest avoiding this. Mainly because you will have much higher monthly payments and if you have not built up the money to cover a down payment other forms of CRE investment might be a better suit for you.

Key Takeaways

What I wanted you to learn from this chapter is how to buy a property. This includes how to properly analyze a market to ensure that there is a future in that city. You do this by analyzing the demographics, supply and demand, as well as capital effects.

You also learned how to find the property itself through many different mediums such as websites, social media, etc.

The last thing you learned was out-of-the-box methods of paying which depended on the individual properties. These methods included getting a real estate license, lease with option to buy, subject to, seller financing, and the seller pays down payment.

There are many ways to buy a property and I wish to guide you to the one that will work the best for you individually.

Something important to take away is that while there were many traditional investment strategies presented before you can still be very creative and work with the previous owner into a deal that will be best for you.

Real estate agents can likely do that very well, but they require a hefty commission and if you do this work yourself very carefully you do not need to worry about human error.

In the end, the most important thing is that you avoid unnecessary risks and enter the field with as much information as possible. If you are unsure about anything there are countless resources available for you including more experienced investors that are always willing to help a rookie.

Remember that critical thinking can get you through any problem you face in this field including property buying. As long as you are very safe about everything you do, you will end up ok.

Chapter 5: Financing

As someone who has authority in this subject, I am very passionate about ensuring that you, my reader, have all the appropriate knowledge needed to be successful.

Mortgages are an integral part of owning properties, and they can decide the fate of hundreds of thousands worth of dollars of your money. A couple of percentages can be the difference between those hundreds of thousands.

This is why I try to teach people around me to be very smart and very careful about everything regarding their mortgage. While the bank you work with usually wants to see you succeed, they also want to get all the money from you as physically possible. So negotiate and any chance you have to refinance for a better deal you need to take it.

What Is Commercial Property Finance?

A large number of variants that encompass commercial property financing, often make it appear unnecessarily intricate and difficult to understand. With all the numerous platforms out there, all applying to specific strategies, the more commonly faced issue is establishing which product is ideal for the needs of your business.

Let's have a look at some of the financing options available and how they work (Funding Options, n.d):

Commercial Mortgages

Commercial mortgages are accessible by a wide range of businesses such as limited companies and sole traders. Generally, lenders are willing to fund as high as 75% of purchase costs, with the maximum number of terms reaching 30 years–typically securing the mortgage against a first charge. Your affordability is assessed and determined by your business's profitability, which provides a forecast of your capacity to successfully make the relevant monthly payments.

Bridging Finance

This option is generally more appealing to investors and property developers as it's a short-term financial solution—it's considered a swift way of financing the purchase of properties. How it works is that the lender will take the first charge on your property and only once your loan has come to term, will they seek an exit.

Auction Finance

This option is structured in consideration of the more experienced landlords and property developers. It entails the arrangement of funding prior to an auction. This means that even before entering the auction room, you'll know what type of property, as well as the property value you can finance.

Portfolio Finance

This applies only to investors with multiple properties under their names. It refers to a long-term business loan where lenders provide you with the option to consolidate borrowing into one loan. This basically means that the various financing you have on your multiple properties are consolidated by the lender and instead of paying on multiple finances, you pay just one large installment. Usability of this option is dependent on rental income.

Mezzanine Finance

Mezzanine finance involves slightly more complex procedures as it's classified as a hybrid form of financing—combining aspects of equity investment and debt financing. It is also secured against the relevant property. This option tends to assist property developers in reducing their cash flow requirements and in turn, enables them to finance projects that ordinarily call for a more significant capital share.

Property Development Finance

This option typically comes in the form of a short-term loan where the funds are utilized either for the renovation or replenishment of an already existing property or the construction and development of a new building project. The maximum number of terms generally applicable to property development financing is 24 months and lenders will advance as much as 70% of the gross development value (Funding Options, n.d).

Commercial Mortgages

How Do These Mortgage Loans Work?

You may be thinking of investing in a property if you plan on expanding your business or the fees relating to commercial rentals are rapidly increasing and are too high. You're likely now willing to explore the various commercial mortgage options available, as a possible business finance source. This is when you'll come to realize that there are quite a few that you may not even have known about.

How to Go About Getting a Commercial Mortgage?

Commercial mortgages eliminate the risks of unexpected increases in rental fees, however, if your finance is set up under a variable rate, monthly repayments could gradually rise. Although, a fixed rate mortgage is also an option for a period of time. Increases in property value cause the business capital to increase as well, and it's important to note that commercial mortgages' interest repayments are tax deductible.

A way to help you meet these monthly repayments is by renting out a section of the property to another business, but this is only possible if such an arrangement is permitted by your lender. Commercial mortgages are considered to be higher-risks which is why the interest rates are slightly higher than that of the residential market, irrespective of the fact that the repayment options are relatively similar. This makes counterbalancing this risk imperative, which can be done by putting down as large a deposit as you possibly can—20% at minimum (Funding Options, n.d).

It's highly recommended to seek advice and assistance from a broker or lender since, in addition to the legal fees, arrangement, and standard valuation costs, there may be additional costs when it comes to commercial mortgages. The current multitude of commercial mortgage providers makes it easy to search and find the most suited company that covers the majority or all of your needs—this includes the leading banks as well as specialist lenders.

Relevant Loan Terms

A loan term refers to the length of time it'll take to fully pay off the loan, through regular disciplined repayments. It's not only applicable to commercial mortgages, this is the case with any form of business finance. Commercial mortgage loan terms can take anything from three years, all the way up to 25 years to be fully paid off.

Commercial loan terms may also refer to the specifications and particulars of the loan, such as the relevant interest rates. They are basically the conditions under which the agreement is being made, which can also be called the Terms and Conditions(Ts&Cs).

How Does One Get a Commercial Mortgage Loan?

The probability of successfully qualifying for a commercial mortgage loan depends on the lender's opinion regarding whether or not your business has the ability to meet the loan repayment terms. You may be requested to provide an in-depth business plan as a means to demonstrate your capacity to fulfill these requirements. Another possibility is the conduction of a professional valuation preceding the securing of a commercial mortgage.

Commercial mortgages are available through leading banks, competitor banks, or specialist lenders. Each may have its own set of terms and may offer different options. Leading banks may necessitate moving your business' banking there for the sake of receiving the maximum benefits or the most beneficial terms. In the case of specialist lenders, you may be offered a mortgage with a lower deposit (interest rates in cases like these tend to be quite steep) or interest-only commercial mortgages.

Commercial Mortgage Deposit

Similarly to when you purchase a home you'd stay in, the commercial mortgage deposit refers to the initial amount of money you pay the lender, which is a certain percentage of the property's full value. The lender then supplies you with a mortgage which enables you to pay for the remaining costs of the property. So, normally, the larger your deposit, the lower your monthly repayment amounts.

How Much Is Need for a Commercial Mortgage Deposit?

Usually, the deposit required for a commercial mortgage is between 25% to 45% of the property's cost. Although, there are various other factors that may contribute to the final figure, as well as the level of potential risk your business may present to the lender. Commercial mortgages where the property is occupied by the owner usually have a 70-80% *loan-to-value*(LTV) ratio. This refers to the extent of your mortgage in relation to the value of the desired commercial property. A commercial mortgage investment's LTV seldomly surpasses 75%, except if the business intends to assign additional security (Funding Options, n.d).

What Is the Average Commercial Mortgage Rate?

Your commercial mortgage rate generally depends on the level of risk and this risk can either increase or decrease, however, this is dependent on the evidence you supply during your application. How the lender prices an application is determined by the size of the loan, LTV, the borrower's credit history and the financials of the business.

It is not limited to these though, as there may be several other factors which influence this price. Generally, using the property as your own business premises tends to offer you a lower interest rate in comparison to if you intend to let it out. Typically, owner-occupied mortgages can range anywhere from 2.25% to 18%. On the contrary, commercial investment mortgages frequently have higher interest rates ranging from 3.5% to 6% (Funding Options, n.d).

It's possible to have either fixed rates or variable rates. Commercial mortgages may have a fixed rate for a length anywhere from two years to the completion of the loan. Commercial mortgages with variable rates follow either LIBOR (London InterBank Offered Rate) or the Bank of England Base Rate.

Lenders

A business loan could be precisely what you need to secure an added investment. It may be the initial start-up of a business enterprise, the improvement of an already existing enterprise (perhaps you just need some new equipment), or a way to finance working capital necessities. This section will inform you of the various kinds of business loans and what they entail, so you can find the finance best suited to your unique business needs.

What Exactly Is a Business Loan?

When you utilize the benefits of a business loan correctly, it can act as a lifeline; however, this requires a clear understanding of how business loans work to make that possible. A business loan usually ranges from £1,000 to a few millions. The terms can be anywhere from one-month repayment plans to 15 years (Funding Options, n.d).

How to Apply?

UK firms are able to access business finance through Funding Options—these options make it possible for businesses and trusted advisors to work closely together. Through funding options, applicants are introduced to a variety of providers and based on each applicant's creditworthiness and circumstances, they are then provided with a quote. All quotes offered by any kind of funding option are dependent on income and status.

Funding Cloud is an award-winning platform, where businesses can swiftly and accurately be matched with the suitable lender and finance option which caters to their specific needs. From a merchant cash advance to revolving credit facilities and unsecured business loans, they work with more than 120 lenders offering a vast number of lending products.

How Much Can a Small Business Loan Get Me?

While the amount that you can borrow depends and differs from lender to lender, your eligibility determines how much you will be able to get out—depending on how much you require. You may be eligible for funding of amounts anywhere between £1,000 to £15M (Funding Options, n.d).

You can either speak to a broker, however, there are numerous business loan calculators available online. One, in particular, is available on Funding Options' website (Funding Options, n.d), where you can establish how much you'd be able to borrow in order to elevate your business. Funding barriers are dissected into an easy application process aimed at empowering the applicant. All partners associated with Funding Options are either registered with the financial ombudsman service or trade public limited companies (bank plc). With revolutionary technology, Funding Cloud (™) accurately validates your business profile and pairs you to the industry's most notable lender network.

Different Types of Business Loans

In general, there are four main types of business loans. The ideal option for your business will depend on your verifiable trading history, cash flow position, and balance sheet assets.

Let's have a look at what these four main types of business loans are (Business Loans, n.d.):

Short-term business loans—Unexpected growth opportunities or Ad Hoc payment demands are quite typical when running a business. This means that you'd require immediate cash. A business owner may consider a revolving credit facility as the best viable option, this way, they'd be able to access this cash. Borrowing of this nature is more suited to occasions where money is required for three months, up to two years. Funding Options has witnessed approvals on eligible borrowers' applications in as quickly as 20 seconds. It's important to note that short-term business loans may offer you quick access to cash, however, the fixed interest rates tend to be higher than normal.

The benefits here are: rapid approvals, funds are made available with little to no delays, increased liberty to seize unanticipated business opportunities and ventures, and less interest payable.

Working capital finance—The working capital loan may be suitable for businesses with short-term expenses, such as rent, stock, and wages. This kind of funding is generally for less than 12 months. Business owners are recommended to try and find lenders who offer tailored Annual Percentage Rate (APR). When you've obtained the estimated repayment terms, you can then easily weigh up the competing rates.

The benefits here are: purchase versatility, no collateral protection, improved cash flow and a swift loan application process.

Unsecured business loans—This loan type doesn't necessitate an offer of security of any kind. *Asset-light* businesses find this option the most attractive, as well as companies that are growing at a quick rate and are in need of growth capital. There are several amazing deals available to business owners because the market is currently very competitive. Unsecured loans reach up to £250,000 and can be utilized for a large number of things, like business expansion or working capital. An important note here is that lenders more often than not, require a personal guarantee.

The benefits here are: management of market uncertainty, ability to purchase necessary items without delays, covers unexpected bills, a quicker means of obtaining funding, much less complicated than secured loans, and access to growth capital for the improvement of your business.

Secured business loans—This option tends to be favored by businesses who operate in *asset-heavy* industries and have prominent trading histories. This kind of loan is often also referred to as asset-backed lending. The nature of this kind of lending requires a business owner to offer assets as a form of security, which can be property, machinery, and plant. The investments the business presents significantly reduce the risk to the lender, which means that the business owner may enjoy better repayment terms and lower interest rates—placing borrowers in a better position to repay the loan over an extended period. Secured loans don't generally necessitate a personal guarantee.

The benefits here are: less rigid credit scores, fixed interest rates, the possibility of early repayment, perfect for short-term financing, better flexibility for SMEs and typically more affordable than unsecured loans.

Property Development Finance

No matter who you are: Investor, landlord, or property developer—there is a range of finance at your disposal to assist in jumping right into your next project. Although, the alternative lending market can make even the most experienced developers feel overwhelmed and a bit confused, so this section aims to help put the most important things into perspective for you, as a means to help you make the most informed decision regarding your property development finance choices.

Property Development Finance UK

Though I mentioned that property finance can be quite complex, even to the most experienced property developers, the advice I am giving you will surely ease the process and equip you with the necessary tools to make the right choices. Whether you want to jump-start an extensive property development project or you just want to refurbish and recondition a buy-to-let property, you will find advice for all business property endeavors, right here.

How Does It Work?

Property development finance refers to the kind of business finance that is used to fund commercial, residential, or mixed-use property developments. This is a relatively broad bracket covering a large variety of financing such as personal loans, bridging loans, mortgages, and term loans. Essentially, it refers to the comprehensive funding of substantive construction or renovation projects. You may even explore this option for the funding of new residential housing works, rejuvenation enterprises, or workspace development. Development finance is probably the most suitable form of property finance for developments being started from scratch.

Private Property Development Finance

Private property finance is your go-to when you find yourself interested in investing in a private residential property but are lacking the immediate funds required. This option is not only available to residential property developers, it's also open to private individuals, building firms, and property organizations.

Once again, the criteria for eligibility vary from lender to lender. Some lenders request detailed business plans while others prioritize your credit score. While numerous other factors can influence your chances of a successful application, having a thorough investment strategy in place will certainly improve your chances of getting an affordable rate.

First-Time Property Development Finance

If you're interested in taking out property development finance, you need to consider a few things beforehand.

To start with, establishing which property development finance option is most applicable to you and your needs, is imperative. For example, if you intend to purchase a property that will be rented out, your ideal finance would be a buy-to-let mortgage.

If you are looking to purchase a new home but have yet to sell your current home, you may prefer a bridging loan. This is also applicable if you'd like to buy a property and renovate it, however, this entails having to pay the full loan amount as well as interest, once the property is sold.

Conducting extensive research of the local market you're planning on purchasing in is crucial before you commit to a property development project. "From scratch," property development finance is designated for larger projects and covers the cost of the grounds and a portion of the construction cost. Property development finance is generally about 70-80% of the cost of building. The developer is expected to obtain the funds for the balance (Funding Options, 2021).

A bridge loan may be the most relevant option if you're intending to undertake short-term renovation projects. This financing option is set up in a manner specific to short-term repayments until the loan can be repaid or a form of longer-term finance can be secured.

Commercial mortgages or longer-term bridging loans are more suited in the case of large renovations.

When the phrase "property finance" does not contain "development" it refers to a variety of financing options pertaining to the property sector. Commercial mortgages, bridging loans, development finance, and auction finance are all forms of property finance.

Building Development Loans

Before you decide to apply for anything, first have a look through all the various building development loans available and what exactly they are typically used for. As soon as you have a clear understanding of what is best suited for you, you can explore your funding options.

Funding Options' team is more than willing to offer you further clarification if you're still a little unsure about what would best suit your needs and circumstances—so don't hesitate to get in touch with them.

Bridging Finance

What Is a Bridge Loan?

This refers to a kind of short-term financing, with terms generally 12 months or less. You are provided with an instant cash boost while you wait for longer-term financing to come through—its purpose is to "bridge the gap," financially. Those who commonly opt for this option are people who are interested in buying a property but still have to sell their current home, as well as several other trade types.

Bridging loans are available through leading banks as well as through finance marketplaces such as Funding Options. It's important to remember that this type of financing is secured with assets such as property—this means failing to meet the repayments would place your home or whichever asset at risk.

How Does a Bridge Loan Work?

Bridge loans are best suited for when you are buying a property whilst waiting for the sale of an existing property to be completed. This means the funds received from the bridge loan can be utilized to cover expenses between the stage of selling the existing property and successfully purchasing the new one. Short-term finance may also be an option if something goes wrong.

Bridging loans can also be used to:

- Cover renovation costs

- Purchase a new home

- Buy to-let mortgage

- Purchase auction properties

- Purchase uninhabitable property

- Purchase land for property development projects

Examples of Bridge Loans

Bridge loans are open to property developers, businesses, and individuals. Below is an idea of what to expect if you fall in the business-minded category and you're planning on relocating to new commercial premises.

- A deposit will be necessary and the remainder will be covered by the borrowed mortgage.

- The company has the funds to pay for the bulk of the deposit; however, it requires additional funds.

- The company still has to wait for the sale of the current property to take place.

- The bridge loan is then taken out in order to "bridge the gap," covering what's left to pay on the deposit.

- The interest and full loan are paid up once the current property has successfully been sold.

The borrower can usually add the loan's monthly interest repayments to the balance of the loan and settle everything together at the end of the term.

Bridge loans are therefore considered quite similar to secured loans, due to the short-term financing nature of this kind of business loan. To qualify for this kind of loan, you will be required to meet the lender's eligibility criteria as well as have a sensible and valid "exit." The *exit* refers to the plan you have in place to repay the loan and interest—this could mean paying everything in full, or transferring it onto a more permanent type of finance such as a mortgage.

It's not uncommon for bridge loans to be used as a quick working capital boost. Start-up companies may visit the bridge loan option while waiting for its equity financing round to close. The funds are then used for operational expenses such as inventory, payroll, utilities, rent, and various other business expenditures.

You may also find businesses who utilize bridge loans to take advantage of time-dependent inventory offers. Owning equity, a sturdy credit history, means by which you can pay off a loan and secure it, often still makes eligibility for a property bridging loan possible—irrespective of a poor credit rating. Your business has to be registered in Wales and England though.

Pros and Cons of Bridge Loans

As with most things in life, there are advantages and disadvantages. The finance industry is no different, so understanding these advantages and disadvantages allows you the ability to weigh them up adequately, and make your decision.

Pros

1. It's quick—A bridge loan offers you quick access to cash as the funds could be ready and available within 24-48 hours. This is significantly quicker than several other term loans.

2. Quantity—The fact that a bridge loan is secured by the borrower's asset means there is a greater chance of borrowing a larger sum of money in comparison to other finance types.

3. Flexibility—This type of loan offers you flexibility when buying a property. Additionally, you also have the choice of variable or fixed interest rates, as well as open or closed loan terms.

Cons

1. Fees—There are other costs to consider such as exit and arrangement fees.

2. Risk—This is also the case with other kinds of secured finance where your property, or whatever other assets, is placed at risk should you be unable to meet the repayments.

3. Higher interest rates—Due to the short-term aspect of this loan, bridge loans generally come with higher interest rates. Unlike other loans where interest is calculated annually, interest on bridge loans is usually calculated monthly.

How Much Do Bridge Loans Cost?

As seen in the cons above, the interest on bridge loans is typically higher than traditional term loans, and on top of that, are calculated monthly as opposed to annually. It depends entirely on the lender whether you would be able to have your interest rates "rolled up," meaning that you will have the ability to pay this when you pay the loan amount at the end of the term.

Be prepared to pay administration and arrangement fees. If you require assistance understanding the terms and conditions of these loans, the Funding Options have a team ready to clarify this for you, so that you can be prepared and know exactly what to expect.

The interest rates on bridge loans can either be fixed or it can be variable, as with most loans. Fixed interest rates offer more consistent monthly repayments as the interest rates remain the same for the duration of the loan term; however, with variable interest rates, the interest rates fluctuate and in turn, so do the repayments. Lenders typically set the variable rate following the Bank of England base rate.

A very important fact to note is that if you still have a mortgage to pay off, you could be looking at paying the bridge loan payment and your mortgage payment until your previous home is sold. While interest may be the main cost, you also need to keep the following in mind:

- Broker fees: Only applicable if you made use of a broker to assist in obtaining bridging finance.

- Arrangement fees: Generally about 1-2% of the total amount borrowed.

- Exit fees: Certain leading banks charge about 1% of the total amount borrowed.

Types of Bridge Loans

Open or Closed:

Open bridge loans mean there is no set date for the loan to be completely paid off, although you are usually expected to have the loan paid off within a year. This option may be ideal if you've already decided on a home you'd like to purchase but still have to sell your current home.

Closed bridge loans on the other hand, have a fixed repayment date. This option is more suitable if you're busy selling a property and expecting to put the money received from that sale, toward the purchase of a new property.

First or Second Charge:

First charge bridging loans refer to the type of loan you get when the property you're securing your loan against has no other loans secured against it.

It will be a *second charge bridge loan* if the property you're securing your loan against already has a loan against it, such as a mortgage.

Variable or Fixed Interest:

With fixed interest rates you'll know precisely how much you're being charged and also have the comfort of knowing that the repayments will remain the same. While variable interest rates are typically less than fixed interest rates, they can change over time.

Auction Finance

This type of finance is a terrific way for property developers to secure below-market-value properties, usually from motivated merchants. If you've got proper expectations from the get-go, this could even be a great option for first-time developers as well.

What Is Auction Finance?

This is a form of bridging loan used for buying properties at auction and assists in completing the purchase process swiftly. Purchasing at auction usually means the transaction needs to be completed within 28 days of the auction, and normally, conventional property purchases are not likely to be completed within such a short period of time. Auction houses request that you pay 10% of the purchase price, as well as additional auction fees—which are payable following a successful bid (Funding Options, n.d).

How to Fund Your Purchase With Property Auction Finance?

For commercial property acquisitions, some financial service providers offer short-term funding. What makes auctions so attractive to buyers is not only how quickly they can be completed, but also because they create a possibility for investors to buy to-let mortgages for a once-off deal, with prospects of generous rental returns.

How Does It Work?

Considering how so many properties lately are clearing six figures in value, even a 10% deposit can be a substantial amount of money. Property auction finance can assist in numerous ways, long before even stepping into the auction itself. Auction finance offers you the freedom of arranging the funds in advance, so you already know what your budget is as well as what specification of the property will be funded by the lender.

Auction finance works as follows (Funding Options, n.d):

Planning and research—This would be the first step in obtaining auction finance. You will be required to research and establish the type of property you'd like to add to your portfolio and locate the relevant auction you'd need to attend.

You can then compile a shortlist of properties you're interested in and proceed to present this to the lender of your choice.

Provisional acceptance—The following step involves going through provisional approval processes of the lender of your choice which may consist of property valuations, credit checks, and income evaluation. This process is relatively straightforward when it comes to experienced developers; however, new property developers need to be a little cautious and not present proposals that are too ambitious—still, they could successfully obtain auction finance. To ensure your goals and plans are realistic and achievable, you may need to consult with a finance professional.

Target selection—This takes place after receiving conditional approval from the lender which means that you'll have to follow certain criteria when buying the desired auction property. For instance, if your finance agreement is that the lender will cover 90% of a 3-bedroom property with a value between £200,000 and £225,000, then that would mean that you'd be responsible for covering the deposit of £20,000. This is just an example and the actual agreement may consist of more specific details, or it may even be more flexible—it all depends on your track record of earlier developments. Having this agreement in place is an essential step before locating potential targets at an auction.

Closing the deal—After having attended the auction and winning the bid on the ideal property, it's now time to pay the deposit. From the day that you've paid the deposit, you'll typically have about 28 days to pay the outstanding balance. This is of course not a concern when you have auction finance in place, as the lender will tend to this payment.

Finalization—Reaching the point of payment of the remaining balance, you can now wait on the finalization of the legal aspect of the purchase. You are expected to make regular contact with your lender, solicitor, and the seller of the property in order to ensure things are progressing appropriately.

How to Get Finance for an Auction Property?

Auctions are considered financially smart ways to purchase real estate, however, the success of this investment is often highly dependent on a satisfactory outcome of the property development project. Although, some people consider this manner of buying riskier in comparison to traditional methods. Because of the speed at which properties are sold, there is little room for due diligence.

A way to protect yourself is by ensuring that the auction house is regulated, registered, and authorized in England and Wales. Auction houses held by the financial conduct authority mean that you can find the company registration number and that they act honestly, effectively and fairly.

Is Auction Finance Right for Me?

This mainly depends on the type of property you are interested in buying. If you're already considering buying a property on auction but your working capital is not available yet, then auction finance could be the best option for you. Auction finance could still be the best option for you if you have positive working capital but you're looking to expand your property portfolio.

Focusing on rampant growth is a key aspect to keep in mind. This is done by keeping your eye on the pattern of data which indicates substantial increases over time. Let's say you invest in beachside areas such as Worthing, Scarborough, and Margate. The housing price increases may help you understand the high appreciation rates in these areas— contrasted to linear markets which face flatter growth over time. Linear markets exhibit easy, stable growth and hardly encounter exceptional spikes or unexpected declines. While peaks and troughs are a less likely occurrence, acquisition prices are much higher and more befitted to established investors who have access to commercial property finance.

For the most part, auction finance provides you with the opportunity to establish or build your property portfolio, irrespective of whether the majority of your capital is locked into your existing properties. In the case of bridging finance, your credit history will more often than not, be one of the main things taken into consideration.

Buying a Property at Auction in the UK

Auctions are an ideal manner in which people can acquire uncommon properties, those that estate agents don't normally sell. With patience and an expert eye, it's easy to find a bargain. The properties you find at an auction can easily be 30% cheaper than those found on the regular market (Funding Options, n.d).

Some of the benefits include (Funding Options, n.d):

- Auction properties tend to have a lower reserve than that of the open market.

- There is less competition.

- Deals aren't terminated as a result of delays.

- Competing bidders can see each other in real-time so they react to counterbids quicker and with more transparency.

- With the current technological advancements, there is more flexibility. A person can now bid by phone, proxy or online.

Is My Business Eligible?

If your business can meet its financial obligations, then yes. There are various lenders offering auction finance to all kinds of businesses like partnerships, sole traders, start-ups, and limited companies. Considering how time-consuming and complex discovering the ideal lender with the most competitive rates can be, seeking professional advice is highly recommended. Funding Cloud has an award-winning, data-driven and innovative platform offering rapid assistance and surety for SMEs through a centralized, two-sided, real-time marketplace that delivers instant choices and solid offers from lenders.

Mezzanine Finance

This is the type of financing that can be considered ideal for management burnouts, large projects or growing businesses. It is commonly described as a hybrid of debt and equity financing and is a fairly convoluted kind of business loan. Businesses that are trying to raise money typically have two basic routes to take.

These are:

- Debt, which is borrowing money using a business loan.

- Equity, which is when you sell a share of your business in exchange for cash.

Mezzanine finance also has the capacity of providing similar benefits to that of property development finance. It covers an assortment of intricate funding scenarios and in some cases, it makes more sense than either equity or debt in their authentic forms.

How Does It Work?

Mezzanine finance is essentially a business loan where the debt turns into an equity share once a pre-agreed timeframe has lapsed. This basically means that should accompany be unable to pay the funding back, the lender acquires a share of equity instead. This is a manner in which the business is used as security.

However, this is not the only form of agreement as mezzanine finance also often blends debt and equity by taking a share of profit and interest payments—this way the business has borrowed the money, and the lender is given a share of the benefits in exchange.

Why Choose Mezzanine Finance?

Mezzanine finance is usually the option on occasions when the deemed risk is so high and the borrower is unable to raise enough money via a traditional business loan. Equity finance is typically the alternative option; however, most companies are hesitant in offering shares in their business. Mezzanine finances make it possible for businesses to borrow large amounts which would be repaid through the profits gained—if everything goes well.

In plain terms, it offers a bigger investment with the intention of a bigger return. Certain situations require lump sum repayments, whereas at other times, interest payments may be postponed. It is also possible for mezzanine finance to have a tax-deductible interest.

These factors all make mezzanine finance slightly different from regular business loans.

The Benefits

It's sometimes used as a sort of "top up" in addition to the amount supplied by the initial lender. For instance, if the initial lender covers 65% of the total you need for the project, mezzanine finance may cover an additional 20%--this leaves the business with only 15% to cover itself. Furthermore, it can also be used as a way to raise more capital with the same amount that you'd be covering yourself, acting as a facilitator for bigger projects which the business wouldn't have been able to afford by itself. This finance intends to allow businesses to achieve maximum returns with the cash contribution available.

Mezzanine Finance for Property Development

Mezzanine development finance can be suitable for property developers as a means to bridge a gap between their deposit and the main property development finance they are going to receive from the funding lender. This offers the developer a way to maximize their returns on investment with fewer upfront costs because they can pay smaller deposits.

In addition to the required deposit, mezzanine finance can be used not only to fill a gap in the deposit but also to enable the developer to save funds for any future deals. Typically, the lender can go as high as covering 90% of the project's costs, which leaves only 10% to the developer.

The lending criteria for property mezzanine finance generally require businesses to prove their experience, as well as present a complete and detailed planning consent which has to be granted. Personal guarantees will also be a necessity. The senior lender may also instruct that Valuation Reports and QS/MS reports be used by and addressed to the mezzanine finance lender.

How Much Does It Cost?

Mezzanine finance is a method where the lender faces more risks as it is secured by a second charge. This means that it has a higher Loan-to-Value, so it's pricier than the senior loan.

Interest rates are specific to the situation and generally start at 12% per annum.

Interest rates are established based on a variety of factors which include market demand, location, deposit input, and a certain amount of finance.

Cash Flow

What Is It?

Cash flow refers to the number of cash-equivalents and cash that flows in and out of your organization. There are numerous ways in which cash can flow into your business, like accounts receivable, or through customers purchasing goods and services. Cash flows out of your business by means of accounts payable and expenses.

A business typically calculates its cash flow monthly, then rolls that figure over every month to keep a record of its business financial prosperity.

Why Does It Matter?

A positive cash flow suggests that the business' liquid assets are increasing, allowing it to pay necessary expenses, meet its debt obligations, and grow with ease. It also signifies that the business has a financial "buffer," which makes it more resilient during difficult times. A negative cash flow, however, suggests that the liquid assets are taking a dip and may require additional financial support if things continue to drop.

Is Cash Flow or Profit More Important?

While cash flow refers to the money flowing in and out of business, profit refers to the money remaining after the business's expenses have been deducted. Cash flow is the funds allowing the business to remain operational whereas profit determines how successful the business is—so managing your business's cash flow is imperative irrespective of high profits.

What Is Cash Flow Forecast?

Calculating cash flow is a good method to keep track of your business finances, however, you can also use this to help predict how much money you'll need. A cash flow forecast provides you with an idea of how much money your company will have in the future, giving you the chance to plan for anticipated peaks or dips in business. It also helps with effective budgeting for new equipment, employees, or stock.

Comparing your cash flow to your cash flow forecast is also useful as it helps you ascertain whether your business is meeting its financial expectations. It also reveals any parts of your business that may require rethinking or revamping to help make it more efficient.

Main Causes of Cash Flow Problems

Numerous things can cause cash flow problems e.g., losses or low profits. This could be as a result of over-investments, waiting on unpaid invoices, or stockpiles. It can also be as a result of seasonal dips in demand or during uncommon occurrences such as global pandemics. Many companies in the UK suffered cash flow problems during 2020, due to the implementation of lockdowns.

How to Avoid Cash Flow Problems?

If your cash flow is causing you concern or you would like to know how to avoid any future issues, there are several things you can do to improve it. This entails managing your stock effectively, accessing credit (if need be), meeting your payment obligations, keeping a regular eye on your cash flow forecast, and restricting unnecessary spending.

Chapter 6: Management

This section is intended to provide you with the knowledge required to make your property sustainable in the long term.

The Right Way to Manage Commercial Properties

Having a solid foundation of facts and knowledge is the most effective way to manage retail and commercial properties. Examining what the issues and facts are is an integral part of the property takeover strategy. It's important to have a clear understanding of all the elements relating to the property as well as the location, as early as possible. A lot of inexperienced property managers know only the basics of what to do, which means they lack the understanding of the broader aspects of property performance and review.

This makes them more likely to overlook critical information which can progress into a huge problem.

All the elements of property should be taken into consideration, such as (Highman, 2017):

- maintenance
- cashflow
- property risk
- tenants

- leases

- occupancy

An adequately planned approach is necessary. Establishing a system of property handover eases the transition into a new property management and tackles all the major issues. This system also helps you avoid omissions and errors during the collection of crucial information. This is why creating a system of property handover is highly recommended.

Establishing Critical Property Facts

As the property manager, it is your responsibility to understand what is considered critical property facts. When it comes to commercial property management and leasing, the tenants and leases form part of the critical factors relevant to the positive cash flow for the landlord. As the landlord, you are required to examine upcoming lease alterations and renewals. These are referred to as "critical dates" and should be followed closely as well as actioned in a timeous manner, as to ensure adherence to the terms of the lease.

It's important to note that many retail or commercial property managers tend to forget, and sometimes don't even bother to identify critical dates. The outcome of such negligence is highly unfavorable as the landlord could potentially face vacancy risk, loss of rental income, or tenant inconstancy.

Some of these critical dates require certain actions to be completed on or before the date mentioned in the lease, so it's imperative that each property manager has a thorough grasp of what their leases entail and you keep your eye on it regularly. Managing numerous clients or properties can therefore be quite demanding and tedious. So, if you're one of the people who's been wondering exactly how many properties are considered too much for one person to handle, keep in mind that there is no straightforward answer to this.

The answer depends on a number of things such as (Highman, 2017):

- landlord reporting needs

- number of tenants

- tenant mix

- maintenance needs

- minimization and vacancy risks

- property marketing necessities

- critical date management

- risk management

- complexity and terms of lease

- type of property (retail is the most time-consuming)

And so forth. Management fees shouldn't be set based on a standard percentage of income; the calculation should be used only to provide you with a base to start from but that's it. All of the issues listed above should be considered before setting a final fee for your property's management services. This brings us back to the importance of having an absolute understanding of your leases and the issues that may arise from them.

Some of the biggest issues and dates relating to leases and tenants under management are (Highman, 2017):

- lease expiration dates

- option dates for new lease terms

- rental reviews and any rental changes in the lease term

- rental payments and recoveries of arrears

- outgoings recoveries and reconciliations

- incentive dates that need impact occupancy or rent

- renovation needs on the part of the tenant

- rental bonds or guarantees influencing rental reviews or rental shifts.

A System of Property Handover

Everyone's checklist may not be the same when it comes to all the elements of a particular property that you should consider—it all depends on leasing, occupancy, and property operations. Since you would have done your research about the town or city in which your property is located, you should have knowledge regarding variables of investment performances that apply to that particular property type. It helps to create a checklist of these elements and as time passes, you may need to refine them.

New management appointments can be daunting and while the below won't cover all the elements that could be relevant to your property, it may help guide you get started. You would then add to this list and apply locational and whatever other factors that may impact your property investment or occupancy more directly.

Cash Flow: It's needless to say that the performance of your investment is reliant on the flow of income from that property. Keep an eye on financial factors relating to change in income and pressure on expenditure. Gather insight into how the net income stream may change as time passes and establish what can be done to improve or enhance the property's life cycle. Cash flow stability should always improve over time, in ways that are relevant and realistic.

Maintenance: You will be required to review the physical features of the property so that you have an idea of how maintenance and repair would work. Keep a keen eye out for elements of risk and damage that could be harmful to public safety or occupancy. Remember that this will always come with insurance risk as it's part of the maintenance review. Take the building's daily functionality and design into consideration and figure out how to remain within the safety and building codes—they may be changed now and then so stay up to date and review things relating to current building code compliance.

Risk Management: It's possible to identify any factors of risk early on and resolve them before they impact the property's financial prosperity. Working closely with maintenance contractors can help you establish where property upgrades and cost controls may occur.

Property Stability: This relies on strategy and awareness. Vacancies may always be troublesome for some properties or landlords, however, there are strategies available to assist with stability. Essentially, it requires an acute balance across tenants, risk management, and leases.

Leases/Occupancy Documents: Because occupancy documents and property leases tend to differ, it's important that you look for the differences. Conduct an in-depth review of all the paperwork and as you go about reviewing them, be sure to record the critical dates and rental information on a diary system or specialized property management software.

The above are just a few of the factors to prioritize as part of the property handover system; however, things like tenancy mix, landlord targets and reporting, and budgeting and forecasting, are additional vital aspects to include in this system. As the property manager, you will be responsible for reviewing all tenants occupying the building and establishing factors affecting vacancy, tenant proximity, and occupancy conflict. You also need to keep your targets and reports in mind, as they will cover expenditure, lease details, income, forecasting, tenant changes and meetings. They basically encompass everything you need to know about your property and its operations.

5 Tips for Successfully Managing Commercial Properties

While commercial properties may share some similarities with residential properties, they come with their own unique challenges. Factors that can negatively impact a property manager's success include *common area maintenance* (CAM), property wear-and-tear, longer leases, and unanticipated emergencies. Thankfully, there are ways in which you can prepare for, prevent, and rectify many of these factors.

They are (Homee Team, 2019):

Know your space

Commercial property managers are expected to have a complete understanding of their industry as well as their commercial spaces. Unlike residential properties, commercial properties are more diverse and need more spatial optimization to account for businesses, renter types, restaurant space, and various other industrial uses. Knowing what your commercial space needs is vital to successful management.

Upgrade regularly

Routine upgrades may sound costly; however, they can impact your bottom line in a highly positive way. Current commercial renters look for updated spaces with improved amenities, therefore updating your space is in the best interest of your company. This doesn't necessarily mean complete renovations—small upgrades can make a huge difference in your tenant satisfaction.

Invest in commercial property software

Because of the considerably large task, it is to manage the plethora of information relating to transactional details and regulations of industrial centers, retail properties, and office spaces, a quality commercial property management software program would take some of that strain off of you as the property manager. It'll help keep your details organized so that revisiting them at a later stage can be done with ease.

Keep tenants happy

With business expansion, the relocation of operations, and various other factors, losing tenants is unfortunately inevitable. Still, keeping tenants is a lot easier than gaining new ones. Creating a safe, positive environment in every single unit is the key to keeping your commercial property full of tenants.

Establish a proactive property maintenance plan

All property managers should prioritize good commercial property maintenance. Reactive approaches to property maintenance refer to basic maintenance and swift and efficient response to emergency maintenance requests, and this by itself is not enough. You require preventative maintenance as it reduces the amount of reactive maintenance you'd have to attend to, which protects your tenants as well as your business.

Chapter 7: Selling Properties

There are various reasons behind a property manager's decision to sell their property and in this chapter, we aim to provide you with the information needed to guide you on how to proceed with this action.

The Process

Selling a commercial property entails a number of steps. After obtaining a buyer, you should expect to do the following (Best, 2019):

1. Communicate with the buyer: Maintaining open communication with the buyer is crucial to a successful sale of the property. This step involves drawing up *Heads of Terms* (HOTS) as well as providing all relevant and necessary information relating to the property such as asbestos surveys and *Energy Performance Certificates* (EPCs).

2. Communicate with solicitors: After supplying your solicitor with your HOTS, they are responsible for obtaining your title documents from the Land Registry. Additionally, your solicitor will be responsible for arranging the exchange of contracts, authorizing any financial transactions, and answering whatever questions you may have related to the sale of your property.

3. Wait for communication between the buyer and seller's solicitors to conclude: This is the stage where contract packages are sent as well as any feedback regarding *Commercial Property Standard Enquiries* (CPSEs).

4. Due diligence: This is a stage that can take weeks to complete and is typically carried out by the buyer's solicitor. You will need to be available for further communication as the buying party may have questions regarding the contract.

5. Negotiate: Once the buyer's solicitor has done their due diligence, there will be documentation to see to; it contains a variety of details including the transfer deeds and terms of sale.

6. Exchange of contracts: The exchange involves the requisite of the buyer to pay a 10% deposit on your property in order to proceed. In exchange, a legally binding completion date is set.

7. Completion: Completion means that your mortgage will now be discharged and the buyer is then the legal owner of the property. This means you hand the keys over and can celebrate the successful sale of your commercial property.

Best Way to Sell Your Commercial Property

Selling a commercial property is a complex process containing various important factors to keep in mind. You are required to have an understanding of legislation surrounding local property values and commercial property sales, as well as an idea of what commercial property buyers may be looking for from sellers.

Preparing to sell

Much like with residential properties, preparing your commercial property for sale is very important. Clutter should be cleared out thoroughly so that the property is tidy and appealing—offering your prospective buyers the chance to envision their business operating from that premises.

Preparing buyer information

Prior to marketing your building, understanding what your buyers could possibly be looking for is another vital part of this process. Typically, their main concerns are the price of the property, suitability, and location. Preparing buyer packs can help the sale along as prospective buyers can find all they need to know in that pack.

The items you should include in the buyer pack are (Rightmove, n.d.):

- commercial energy performance certificates (EPC)

- lawful use certificates, planning permissions, and use classes

- details for stamp duty land tax, business rates, and whatever other costs the buyer will be responsible for

- if applicable: asbestos survey

If you need more information on what your buyer information pack should contain, you can speak to your commercial agent.

Employing a commercial agent

Choosing a commercial agent who is a member of an accredited trade body such as the Royal Institution of Chartered Surveyors (RICS), is highly recommended. The reason is that all creditable agents have personal insurance. This covers the seller's damages should they receive negligent advice. Before looking to market your property, a commercial agent usually provides you with a detailed valuation report.

Solicitors

In addition to a commercial agent, you will require a solicitor. Solicitors are responsible for a number of processes during the commercial sales process. Their duties include arranging the exchange of contracts, supervising any deposits, answering questions you may have, and confirming successful transfers of monies. Choosing the right solicitor is imperative for a swift and efficient sale.

Marketing your property

Your property can be marketed through an agent of your choice as long as they have a clear understanding of what you are expecting from the sale, so provide your agent with the relevant information needed to assist in marketing your property. Their in-depth knowledge and experience will then allow them to add to your information with detailed descriptions and photographs, to maximize your chances of success.

Selling costs

Irrespective of the type of property you're selling, warehouse or office, you need to remember that there are costs attached to it.

These costs include:

- Capital gains tax—your solicitor can help you establish if the sale of your investment property has made you liable for any capital gains tax.

- Solicitor fees—gather a number of quotes and compare them as solicitors typically have a fixed fee for their conveyancing services.

- Commercial agent fees—due to the competition commercial agents generally have with each other, they don't tend to change their fees much. Still, you'd much rather discuss those fees before instructing them to sell your property.

- Removal costs—if your commercial property has furniture, equipment, or other assets which do not fall part of the sale present at the property, you will be required to arrange for the removal of those goods at your own cost.

- Mortgage redemption fee—if your commercial property still has a mortgage and you intend to pay this off early, you may be liable for a mortgage redemption fee.

- Mortgage arrangement fee—the inability to transfer your existing mortgage, for whatever the reason may be, could leave you liable for a mortgage arrangement fee for any new mortgages you may need.

Property Value

The amount a commercial property is worth is dependent on various factors.

Such as:

- Market trends

- Availability of like properties

- Condition of your property

- Value of recently sold properties in the surrounding areas

Accepting an offer

Your commercial agent should be in charge of all offers you receive. They are legally required to inform you of any offers. Your agent will formally inform you of any offers; however, if you are presented with multiple offers, consider the following points as a means to assist you in figuring out which buyer would be the more suited option.

- The financial status and position of the buyer.

- Whether they have a mortgage offer or already have one in place.

- Whether they are a mortgage or cash buyer.

Accepting an offer takes you to the next step, which is the draft of a Sale Agreement which you as well as the purchaser will have to approve.

Exchange of contracts and completion

After the exchange of contracts, your buyer will then pay a deposit to the solicitor and a date for completion will be decided upon. All legal factors of the sale are completed on the day of completion and the mortgage lender will release the remaining funds to the solicitor.

This is the general procedure of a typical commercial sales process; however, remember that each sale is different and the process may differ slightly, depending on the nature of the sale.

The Right Time to Sell Your Property

Selecting the right time to sell your commercial property can have an enormous impact on the success of your sale. Determining the ideal time for a sale such as this is crucial to getting the most out of your property's sale.

According to the president of Bull Realty Inc, Michael Bull, commercial property values continue to be periodic. Commercial property marketing consists of 4 phases which are: Recession, Recovery, Expansion, and Contraction. Establishing which phase the market is in is useful in determining whether selling your commercial property at that specific time is wise (Movehut, n.d.).

The Recession Phase is considered the worst time to sell your commercial property because property prices are at their lowest and financing availability becomes unaffordable to the vast majority. Consequently, this results in the loss of tenants and commercial property owners have trouble finding occupiers. If you can avoid the worst phase of the cycle, you can limit the loss of capital or profit. With that said, this phase may be an opportune time for buyers to secure prime locations.

Financing becomes affordable again during the Expansion stage and it encourages stronger bids and higher selling prices. It may be harder for buyers to secure properties they really want during this stage because the competition with other commercial property investors who are pursuing the same properties, is higher at this point.

Selling decisions should be based on need during the other two phases.

Either way, it is recommended that you seek professional advice from a commercial agent as they will help you identify if the yield curve is expanding or contracting—this has a direct influence on corresponding property values.

Conclusion

We've now learned more than simply the basics of commercial real estate and have established that it can fit pretty much any type of person. Whether you are good with your hands and can fix structural issues without the need for contractors, or whether you are a research specialist and can adequately examine location growth and the administration that goes into commercial real estate; your skill set remains useful. The aspects where you are lacking knowledge and experience will then be the only parts you may need professional assistance with—and there is no shame in seeking professional advice.

Remember that commercial real estate Is considered a passive income, however, the majority of efforts are required to be put in from the very start, before purchasing your commercial property and only thereafter, does the effort slightly decrease. You've seen that in no way does this mean your work ends once you've successfully purchased it, to maximize your profits and ensure the success of your business, actively being involved and informed is what separates a surviving business from a thriving business.

Don't allow yourself to be so eager to jump right in that you ignore the steps mentioned in this book. All of these facts and factors have been added for a reason and that reason is to help guide you to prosperity in your investment. As mentioned in Chapter 1, your first and most important step will always be the classification of the commercial property you're looking to buy. Not only does it require classification but you also need to weigh up the advantages and disadvantages and understand how suitable it is for your capacity, plans, and your life.

Another crucial point to take with you is that while I'm able to offer you the best of my knowledge and guidelines, every single property has its own unique implications and challenges, advantages and disadvantages, and as the prospective investor, it'll be your responsibility to do thorough research and brainstorming before buying land that is best suited to you. Some properties may have fewer implications than others so remain focused on what you want out of that property and your final decision should be a property that ticks most, if not all, of your boxes. This is your "due diligence" and you will never regret this step.

And finally, now knowing how important mortgages are in owning commercial properties, your business decisions, improvements, and alterations should all positively affect your cash flow and profits so that your mortgage payments are made one time. Stability here will open so many doors for new development projects and your property portfolio will be your key to continue growing and expanding your investments.

Discussion Section

Here are a few things worth mentioning again:

A. Finding the ideal property relies heavily on the quality of your due diligence.

B. There are numerous platforms out there for all kinds of projects, you just have to do your homework to find the best one for yours.

C. Commercial properties have unique management priorities and attending to these needs effectively and quickly is yet another essential key to the success of your investment.

If you enjoyed reading this book, please go ahead and leave a review on Amazon. Your thoughts and opinions are more than welcome!

References

Best, D. (2019, January 7). *Selling Commercial Property*: What Do I Need To Know? Savoy Stewart. https://www.savoystewart.co.uk/blog/selling-commercial-property

Cauble, T. (2020a, April 20). *How to Passively Invest in Commercial Real Estate*. The Cauble Group. https://www.tylercauble.com/blog/how-to-passively-invest-in-commercial-real-estate

Cauble, T. (2020b, June 3). *How to Raise Investment Capital for Commercial Properties*. The Cauble Group. https://www.tylercauble.com/blog/how-to-raise-capital-for-commercial-properties

Cauble, T. (2020c, July 8). *How to Analyze Commercial Real Estate Deals*. The Cauble Group. https://www.tylercauble.com/blog/how-to-analyze-commercial-real-estate-deals

Funding Options. (n.d.-a). *Auction finance for property acquisition in the UK*. Funding Options. Retrieved July 19, 2022, from https://www.fundingoptions.com/knowledge/auction-finance

Funding Options. (n.d.-b). *Bridging Loan & Bridging Finance*. Funding Options. https://www.fundingoptions.com/knowledge/bridging-loans-bridging-finance

Funding Options. (n.d.-c). *Business loans. Funding Options.* https://www.fundingoptions.com/knowledge/business-loans#lenders

Funding Options. (n.d.-d). *Cash flow for business owners.* Funding Options. https://www.fundingoptions.com/knowledge/cashflow

Funding Options. (n.d.-e). *Commercial mortgage guide.* Funding Options. https://www.fundingoptions.com/knowledge/commercial-mortgage

Funding Options. (n.d.-f). *Commercial property finance.* Funding Options. https://www.fundingoptions.com/knowledge/commercial-property-finance

Funding Options. (2021). *Property Development Finance Explained.* Funding Options. https://www.fundingoptions.com/knowledge/property-development-finance

Gifford, C. (2011, February 18). *Tracker funds explained.* Which? Money. https://www.which.co.uk/money/investing/types-of-investment/investment-funds/tracker-funds-explained-a6s543x0ss5x#headline_6

Gifford, C. (2014, May 27). *Fund supermarkets: compare customer satisfaction.* Which? https://www.which.co.uk/money/investing/investment-platforms/investment-platforms-reviewed/best-and-worst-investment-platforms-anyxw2k9cdz8

Highman, J. (2013, May 2). *Watch for Critical Dates and Lease Issues in Commercial Real Estate.* Commercial

Real Estate Training Online. https://commercial-realestate-training.com/watch-for-critical-dates-and-lease-issues-in-commercial-real-estate/

Highman, J. (2017, October 13). *The Right Ways to Manage Commercial Properties.* Commercial Real Estate Training Online. https://commercial-realestate-training.com/the-right-ways-to-manage-commercial-properties/

Homee Team. (2019, October 14). *5 Tips for Successfully Managing Commercial Properties.* Homee. https://www.homee.com/blog/tips-for-successful-commercial-property-management

Kaveh, K. (2011, February 18). *Investment trusts explained.* Which? https://www.which.co.uk/money/investing/types-of-investment/investment-trusts/investment-trusts-explained-agmsw3f4fnqq

Movehut. (n.d.). *Choosing the Right Time to Market Your Commercial Property.* Movehut. https://www.movehut.co.uk/commercial-property-guides/commercial-property-selling-guide/choosing-the-right-time-to-market-your-commercial-property

Newman, J. (2016, November 13). *Due diligence checklist for commercial real estate acquisitions.* Thompson Coburn. https://www.thompsoncoburn.com/insights/publications/item/2016-11-13/due-diligence-checklist-for-commercial-real-estate-acquisitions

Paul Mall Estates. (n.d.). *Types of Commercial Lease.* Pall Mall Estates.

https://www.pallmallestates.co.uk/resource/types-of-commercial-lease/

Property News Team. (2019, May 2). *Guide to buying commercial property.* Zoopla. https://www.zoopla.co.uk/discover/buying/guide-to-buying-commercial-property/

Reonomy. (2019, October 17). *The 8 Types of Commercial Real Estate.* Reonomy. https://www.reonomy.com/blog/post/types-of-commercial-real-estate

Richardson, D. (2010, April 1). *Capital gains tax on shares.* Which? https://www.which.co.uk/money/tax/capital-gains-tax/capital-gains-tax-on-shares-ambbh8b4kuxt

Rightmove. (n.d.). *Selling a commercial property.* Rightmove Guides. https://www.rightmove.co.uk/guides/seller/other-things-to-consider/selling-a-commercial-property/

Rogan, E. (n.d.). *How to Analyze a Commercial Real Estate Deal.* Penn Capital Group. https://penncapitalgroup.com/education/how-to-analyze-a-commercial-real-estate-deal/

Saracens Solicitors. (2013, March 19). *Landlord and Tenant Relationships - Commercial Property.* Saracens Solicitors. https://saracenssolicitors.co.uk/business-clients/commercial-property/to-trust-or-not-to-trust-landlord-and-tenant-relationships-commercial-property/

Sonntag, D. (2021, March 8). *Properties & Pathways - A due diligence checklist for buying commercial property.* Properties & Pathways.

https://propertiesandpathways.com.au/commercial-property-due-diligence-checklist/

The Cauble Group. (n.d.). *Buy Commercial Property With No Money.* The Cauble Group Commercial. https://www.tylercauble.com/blog/buy-commercial-propertywith-no-money

The Cauble Group. (2020, May 25). *5 Reasons You Should Forget Residential Investing.* The Cauble Group. https://www.tylercauble.com/blog/commercial-vs-residential-real-estate#

Trudeau, M. (2016, August 2). *Commercial property investment explained.* Which? Money. https://www.which.co.uk/money/investing/how-investing-works/asset-classes-explained/commercial-property-investment-explained-awzg31j6bwpz

Which? Money. (2011, February 18). *Unit trusts and OEICs explained.* Which? https://www.which.co.uk/money/investing/types-of-investment/investment-funds/unit-trusts-and-oeics-explained-alfnz3k6nt5f

Which? Money. (2015, April 5). *What is a stocks and shares Isa?* Which? https://www.which.co.uk/money/investing/stocks-and-shares-isas/what-is-a-stocks-and-shares-isa-al4902u4yqgg

Which? Money. (2022, April). *Building an investment portfolio.* Which? https://www.which.co.uk/money/investing/how-investing-works/building-an-investment-portfolio

Printed in Great Britain
by Amazon